Instructor's Manual
to Accompany

The Aims of Argument

Second Edition

Carolyn E. Channell
Timothy W. Crusius

Southern Methodist University

Mayfield Publishing Company
Mountain View, California
London • Toronto

International Standard Book Number: 0-7674-0028-3

Manufactured in the United States of America
10   9   8   7   6   5   4   3   2   1

Mayfield Publishing Company
1280 Villa Street
Mountain View, CA 94041

Contents

Preface

We encourage all instructors teaching with *The Aims of Argument,* whether new or experienced, to make some use of this Instructor's Manual. Even those who have taught argument for many years will find it helpful for taking full advantage of the text's innovative approach. This manual is designed to accompany both *The Aims of Argument: A Rhetoric and Reader* and its briefer counterpart, *The Aims of Argument: A Brief Rhetoric.*

Part One of the manual introduces each of the chapters in Part One of the text, beginning with a discussion of the theory or theories that guided us in our conception of that chapter, followed by more specific suggestions for using the chapter in the classroom. Sample responses to the Following Through exercises, especially helpful to new teachers, can be found at the end of each of the chapters in Part One. These responses should be regarded as suggestions; in almost every case, different responses are possible.

In Part Two, we offer possible responses to the questions following each of the readings in Part Two of the text. It is not our intention to advocate a particular position, only to show one or two possible directions for thinking about and discussing the issues raised.

Part Three offers responses to some of the practice exercises in Appendix B.

We want to thank our colleague Gary Kriewald for his contribution to this manual and the editor of the first edition, Jan Beatty, for anticipating better than we could the needs of teachers who will be using *The Aims of Argument* for the first time.

Carolyn E. Channell
Timothy W. Crusius
Southern Methodist University

Part One: The Aims of Argument

Chapter 1
An Overview of the Text

THE AIMS APPROACH

This text is based on the idea that argument is a means to an end, and it focuses on four aims, or purposes, to which argument is most often employed: as a means to *inquire* into an issue or position; as a means to *convince* others of the merit of a position; as a means to *persuade* others not only to accept an opinion but to act upon it in some way; and as a means to *negotiate* or mediate between conflicting positions.

The advantages of focusing on aims are numerous. Most argument texts focus on the components of an argument. In such texts, students find chapters on structure; on logic (syllogisms, enthymemes, induction); on audience; on evidence; on categories of arguments, such as arguments based on definition or on cause and effect; even on fallacies—what not to put into an argument. We have found that students using such texts have difficulty seeing how all the discrete things they learn *about* argumentation coalesce in actual discourse. Too often, they see learning argument (or worse, its terminology and parts) as an end in itself.

Our aims approach, however, is holistic and realistic, having its roots in discourse theory. In *A Theory of Discourse,* James Kinneavy defines discourse as a process "characterized by individuals acting in a special time and place"; as having "a beginning, a middle, a closure, and a purpose" within a "situational and cultural context" (22). Every chapter in *The Aims of Argument* is concerned with the whole of an argument rather than a part, and in each case we situate the argument rhetorically: Whether they are reading arguments or writing their own, students see that the content or message of a text cannot be viewed in isolation from the motives and strategies of a particular speaker addressing a particular audience. We believe that the aims approach enables students to see how each of the topics covered in the book is part of the process of creating an argument for a real-life purpose.

Kinneavy's theory imposes order on the vast field of discourse analysis by discriminating categories of discourse according to aim. As he explains, the aim or purpose of a discourse determines everything else: "Sounds, morphemes, syntactic patterns, meanings of all kinds, skills in speaking and the other arts of discourse, narratives and the other modes of discourse—all of these exist so that humans may achieve certain purposes in their use of language with one another. Both a theory of language and a theory of discourse, then, should be crowned with a viable framework of the uses of discourse" (37–38).

We believe that a useful order can be imposed on the study of argument by identifying purposes that people attempt to achieve through argument, and by showing how these aims determine the choices people make when creating arguments. The aims approach gives to a course in argument an elegantly simple structure with clear pedagogical advantages. Experience has convinced us that students learn best when they can see how the material presented in lecture or a text fits into a larger scheme or pattern. By identifying four aims for making arguments and offering a rationale for sequencing them as we have, the introduction to the text provides students with just such a pattern.

Each of the "Aims" chapters (Five through Eight) situates its topic within this scheme, suggesting how students can relate the material about to be presented to what they have already learned. Students should have no trouble seeing that aims can overlap, and in fact this allows some helpful recursiveness as the semester progresses.

In designing this sequence, we have integrated oral and written discourse. Our first aim, inquiry, draws upon the tradition of Platonic dialogue, which had as its goal the discovery of truth. (For us, however, truth is not objective but intersubjective; ours is a linguistically constructed truth.) We want students to see that this aim is best accomplished through the give and take of ordinary conversation, but we make reading and writing part of the process of inquiring. We show how the dialogue of inquiry can and should be part of the process of making arguments to convince and to persuade, which are written monologues. Finally, our fourth aim, negotiation, returns to dialogue, but we show how writing can assist in the process of resolving conflict.

We and our colleagues at Southern Methodist University who have tested *The Aims of Argument* in the classroom have found that students like this book because the material is presented in a consistent and logical fashion. But to teach writing, no textbook can suffice. A teacher, interacting with students in classroom and conference, is obviously crucial.

The Aims of Argument is a text that invites students to think. It does less *telling* than *showing* and *asking*. We hope that as you and your students proceed through the text, you will find that your role as teacher is not to explain the text, but rather to engage with students in the activities presented in each chapter. For those using the text for the first time, this manual shows what is likely to happen along the way.

A PROCESS APPROACH: THE CLASSROOM AS WRITING WORKSHOP

Since we prefer a workshop atmosphere in our classrooms, we have written a text that facilitates student activity and interaction. Each chapter focuses on some process (for example, how to read an argument, how to inquire, how to convince). Students need two to three weeks to work through the stages of each major writing project; some projects may take a month. Students are impatient and tend to procrastinate, and they are probably used to taking no more than an evening to write their high school papers and papers for other courses. In our courses, they have to work more thoughtfully through the process.

Generally, the chapters first model the process and then guide students through a writing project of their own. Both modeling and guiding sections contain Following Through exercises designed to keep students interacting with text, teacher, and peers. Parts of the process of writing the major essays take place in the classroom, preventing students from skipping or putting off the essential steps of prewriting and drafting, and allowing the teacher to intervene as necessary. Following are some suggestions for what to do in class.

In-class writing. We don't expect students to produce a finished essay in a class period, but students should accept the idea that in a writing class, one may be asked to write. Examples of in-class writing projects include the following.

1.   Short "free-writings" in which grammar, spelling, and organizational problems don't count. This is an excellent way to reinforce the main points of a reading

assignment and to reveal where students need more help with a concept. In more practical terms, it holds students responsible for keeping up with their reading and for attending class regardless of whether you give grades or simply "credit." Ask an open-ended question about the reading, have students apply a concept from the reading, or assign one of the Following Through exercises. We have found that "warm-up" writings such as these at the beginning of class do, in fact, help students better recall what they read, enabling them to participate more fully in class discussion.

2. Collaborative writings. Much current composition research points to the value of collaborative learning. We have found that if you ask students to do a short writing assignment as homework (such as an analysis, a paraphrase, a summary, a dialogue), they welcome the chance to work in pairs, creating a revision based on the best of both efforts. In a small class of 15 or 18, with a displayed computer screen, we have even asked the entire class to participate in revising a paragraph or writing a dialogue.

3. Peer editing. Students in our classes exchange drafts and write responses to each other's work. We suggest that you model this activity for students in one class period before asking them to undertake it themselves in another. We also suggest that you hand out printed guidelines listing things they should be looking for, similar to the checklists at the end of Chapter 6 on convincing and Chapter 7 on persuading. We have found that giving students grades on their peer editing encourages them to be more discerning critics.

Sharing drafts throughout the writing process. Many students are reluctant to do this at first, but once the class gets used to exchanging papers and everybody sees that no one's writing is perfect, they begin to want this experience. We have students competing to have their drafts reproduced or projected so that the whole class may critique them.

Student presentations. Students need experience speaking in public. They also need opportunities to take responsibility for their own learning. Oral presentations achieve both these goals. For example, you might ask students to "present" their analysis of a published argument, based on some aspect of the critical reading guidelines in Chapter 3 or of Toulmin's scheme in Chapter 4, or to pair up and prepare a dialogue for presentation to the class. Any time you can turn the tables on students and require them to do what they assume is your job, you will find they learn more. Be careful to be specific about the assignment and the standards you will hold students to. There is nothing worse than an unprepared student taking up class time.

USING THE TEXT THROUGH THE SEMESTER

We teach a 15-week semester, with classes meeting three times a week for 50 minutes, or twice a week for 90 minutes. The following suggestions are based on that schedule, but we include an outline for a shorter course as well. Depending on the abilities of our students, we assign three or four major writing assignments along with many smaller projects, most of which lead up to one of the major essays. Each writing project focuses on a different aim, and we make writing, not reading, the center of the course. While many new teachers enjoy reading and discussing professional essays—

whether in the reading section of a rhetoric text or in a supplemental reader—our experience cautions us that it is better to deal with fewer readings and analyze them closely, especially in terms of how they relate to the actual writing project students are working on.

One Route through the Text

When we use this text, we organize the semester around Part One, moving from Chapter 1 to Chapter 8. (See the Sample Syllabus later in this chapter of the manual.) Because the material and skills presented in Part One build cumulatively, we ask students to revisit certain pages in the early chapters even as we venture into the later ones. It is entirely possible to delete some chapters or parts of chapters in Part One, as we will explain.

Our route through the text takes constant detours into both the Part Two readings and the Appendices. Students write arguments on topics selected from Part Two, so they use the readings in one of the chapters there as a first resource for surveying an issue. Visits to parts of Appendix A: Researching Arguments can begin along with any of the chapters in Part One. For example, students may look to the advice there on paraphrasing and summarizing while they are working through Chapter 3: Reading an Argument. Since we believe students need to do research to argue responsibly on most current issues, we always assign this material by the time they argue to convince in Chapter 6. Appendix B: Editing and Proofreading is assigned just before the first major essay is due.

Our rationale for following the Part One sequence is that its order suggests a process for writing responsible arguments and it enables us to integrate reading and writing throughout, emphasizing their complementary roles. From the first week—even the first day—of class, students can begin working on a major writing project, and they can see how everything they learn about keeping a notebook, reading and analyzing arguments, doing research, and so forth applies directly and immediately to that project.

Sample Syllabus

The following syllabus illustrates one way to use *The Aims of Argument* in a 15-week semester.

Weeks 1 and 2

Goals: To introduce the concepts of rhetoric, argument, and the aims; to teach critical reading skills.

Reading: Chapter 1: An Overview of Key Terms
Chapter 2: Keeping a Writer's Notebook
Chapter 3: Reading an Argument
Professional essays from Part Two

Writing: Notebook entries, as suggested in text

Weeks 3 through 5

Goals: To acquaint students with the skills, methods, and criteria required for evaluating the quality of arguments. (Optional goal: To show students how to synthesize and evaluate a range of positions in published arguments.)

Reading: Chapter 4: Analyzing an Argument: A Simplified Toulmin Method
Chapter 5: Preparing to Write: Arguing to Inquire
Professional essays from Part Two

Writing: A dialogue with the author of a published argument, an evaluative analysis of an argument, or an exploratory essay

Weeks 6 through 9

Goals: To teach students how to argue to convince, with emphasis on the case structure of thesis, reasons, and evidence; to teach students how to use the library to research an issue; to teach students how to paraphrase, summarize, take notes, and write annotated bibliographies; to teach students how to draw from source material and incorporate sources into their own writing; to teach students the process of drafting, revising, editing, and proofreading an argument.

Reading: Chapter 6: Making Your Case: Arguing to Convince
Appendix A: Researching Arguments
Appendix B: Editing and Proofreading
Professional essays from Part Two (optional, because students will be doing research)

Writing: Paraphrases, summaries, notecards, and an annotated bibliography
An argumentative essay to convince

Weeks 10 through 12

Goals: To teach students how to draw upon the full range of rhetorical appeals when aiming to persuade a specific audience of readers.

Reading: Chapter 7: Appealing to the Whole Person: Arguing to Persuade
Professional essays from Part Two

Writing: Audience profile
An argumentative essay to persuade

Weeks 13 through 15

Goals: To teach students how to analyze conflicting arguments to find possible areas of common interest; to teach students strategies for resolving conflict.

Reading: Chapter 8: Negotiation and Mediation: Resolving Conflict
Professional essays from Part Two

Writing: A mediatory essay

Alternative Routes

Some teachers may wish to take a slower pace than the one described by the syllabus above. If you choose to eliminate one of the four aims, it should probably be negotiation (Chapter 8) since the other three aims are practically prerequisites if students are to complete the Chapter 8 assignment successfully. As there is some overlap between Chapters 3 and 4, teachers who want to spend less time on analysis could go directly from Chapter 3 to Chapter 5. Teachers who want to focus their courses on convincing and persuading can eliminate the negotiation chapter and opt not to assign a major writing project stemming from the inquiry chapter. However, because understanding the modes of inquiry is essential to most research, you should assign the pages that explain the concept (pp. 42–44), that list the questions for inquiry (pp. 44–45), and that contain the sample dialogues illustrating inquiry into a written text (pp. 46–52) and peer inquiry (pp. 71–73).

OPTIONS FOR WRITING ASSIGNMENTS

A writing course should be organized around writing projects. *The Aims of Argument* opens up a range of options not only of topics for these assignments, but also of forms that these assignments can take.

With respect to topics, some teachers in our program choose one topic (or even one issue) for the class to explore through the entire semester. (Or they allow the class to choose from among the topics covered in the readings section.) This single-topic option takes the most economical advantage of the cumulative nature of Part One. If students write an argument to persuade on a topic that they have already explored and written about as they worked through the chapters on inquiry and convincing, they have much less new groundwork to lay before beginning to draft. It also allows students to work collaboratively, compiling a common bibliography, inquiring into each other's positions, and giving informed peer critiques. The disadvantage, obviously, is that some students may exhaust their interest or never have a genuine interest in the chosen topic. Still, this option makes sense for a five-week summer semester or for a class of basic writers, who benefit especially from close attention.

Generally, we prefer to offer students more variety. Whether they are analyzing arguments or writing their own, we begin with a common topic, then let students choose their topics individually for the later assignments. We have found, however, that the negotiation chapter works best if the whole class focuses on the range of positions on a single issue.

The Aims of Argument offers teachers considerable flexibility in assigning writing projects. While the chapters on convincing and persuading take students through the process of writing fairly traditional argumentative essays, the chapters on inquiry and negotiation offer some alternatives, such as dialogues and evaluative analysis papers.

SUGGESTIONS FOR TEACHING

We make this chapter the first reading assignment, and we discuss it at the second class meeting. It is essential that students understand the concept of aims, the idea that argument is positive and constructive, and the definition of rhetoric. In class discussion, you may wish to bring in some letters to the editor and ask your students to decide on a dominate aim for each. You may ask students to write an in-class response to the Following Through on page 10.

Bibliography

Corbett, Edward P. J. *Classical Rhetoric for the Modern Student.* 3rd ed. New York: Oxford UP, 1990.

Kinneavy, James L. *A Theory of Discourse.* New York: Norton, 1980.

Chapter 2
Teaching the Writer's Notebook

THE GOALS FOR CHAPTER 2

Quite simply, we want students to acquire the habit of keeping a notebook and to take responsibility for using it in a variety of ways. While they are accustomed to keeping a notebook to record lecture notes in all their other classes and may have had to keep a journal in high school, they probably have not seen their notebooks as a place for recording, analyzing, prewriting, inventing, keeping research notes, and simply responding to their reading assignments.

SUGGESTIONS FOR TEACHING

Asking students to keep a notebook presents teachers with a certain dilemma: If we require students to fill a certain number of pages per week and collect the notebooks or check them periodically, students perceive the whole endeavor as busywork; if we suggest that they keep a private notebook because many real writers do so, many will fail to take the initiative.

We think our approach offers a way out of this dilemma. By letting students choose the type of notebook or folder they are most comfortable with and by not collecting them, teachers suggest that the notebook is the student's responsibility. However, after reading this chapter, students will see that the notebook has numerous practical purposes, and teachers can reinforce this point in several ways:

1. Keeping a writer's notebook of their own, and sharing with their students some of the entries. For example, you could write your own responses to some of the Following Through exercises and read them in class before asking students to read theirs.

2. Requiring students to bring the writer's notebook to class, where they may use it to record information and ideas gathered from class discussions.

3. Asking students to bring their writer's notebook to office conferences. We use the writer's notebook to work out thesis sentences, diagram cases, and take notes about suggestions and ideas that come up in the conference. In a post-grading conference, we often will write into the notebook a mini-lesson on some point of grammar, punctuation, coherence, and so forth, geared to the individual student's writing problems on the graded paper.

4. Asking students to do the various Following Through exercises in their writer's notebook and then having them report to the class on what they wrote about.

5. Asking students to write their responses to questions about the readings in their writer's notebook, facilitating class discussion.

ANSWER TO FOLLOWING THROUGH EXERCISE

Page 15: This is an open-ended question. We suggest you write a notebook entry of your own, listing some possible topics you might want to write an argument on, and develop one or two of these with reasons and an intended audience.

Chapter 3
Teaching Critical Reading

THE GOALS FOR CHAPTER 3

This chapter presents a process of reading aimed at counteracting the common undergraduate view that reading ability means being able to move through a text quickly to find out what it says. Students often look through a text as they would a window; they are unaccustomed to considering why or how the text says what it does.

Here we model a method that draws attention to the context of an argument, its structure, and specific rhetorical features. We also invite students to argue with the text, in a dialogue in the margins that is a preview of the art of inquiry. All of these activities take time, especially for the uninitiated. Therefore, for pedagogical reasons, we suggest three separate readings of any argument, each with its respective purpose. Obviously, as student readers become more skilled, these purposes will merge into any single reading. However, students will still see how multiple readings of a text open it to their understanding and appreciation.

Our textbook slows the reading process down to this extent because we believe attention to these skills carries over into writing, and because we believe that students need to read *rhetorically*, whether they are analyzing a single text as this chapter illustrates, or researching a topic through an examination of multiple sources. Doug Brent explains the value of teaching rhetorical reading as part of preparing students to write a researched argument:

> A common image of the research process, that it is simply a means of acquiring data, does not encourage teachers to teach [the] skills of active construction and evaluation. . . . The goal of instruction must be to help students get research back inside the rhetorical act, a place where more experienced readers (whether or not they consciously know it) routinely place it. Students must learn to see the texts that intervene between them and the subject of their research as more than repositories of data that "maintain a solemn silence" when questioned [Socrates' complaint about writing in Plato's *Phaedrus*]. . . . They must learn to see them as repositories of alternate ways of knowing . . . which must be actively interrogated and whose meaning must be constructed, not simply extracted. (104–105)

The Aims of Argument consistently approaches reading with this emphasis on careful, even methodical, interrogation—not only in this chapter but also in Chapter 4, on using the Toulmin method to analyze an argument; in Chapter 5, which illustrates a dialogical approach to inquiry into written texts; and in Appendix A, which explains how students should evaluate the sources they encounter when doing research.

SUGGESTIONS FOR TEACHING

This chapter takes students through a very detailed process of reading an essay by Anna Quindlen. We suggest that rather than assigning the whole chapter for homework, you use at least some class time to begin this assignment, asking students to respond in their writer's notebooks to the Following Through exercises on page17.

Analyzing Structure

Breaking any lengthy text into its major subdivisions is an activity students quickly see the value of, yet have seldom been asked to do. Instead of seeing a text as a series of individual paragraphs, they discover how paragraphs work together to develop a portion of the argument. Students recognize that this skill not only helps them recognize the structure of a given argument but also carries over to help them develop and organize their own longer pieces of writing.

Our discussion of reading to see how the parts of an argument function (pp. 20–22) is heavily indebted to Kenneth Bruffee's "descriptive outline," as described in *A Short Course in Writing*. For each paragraph, Bruffee has students write:

1. A "says" statement, which summarizes the content of the paragraph.

2. A "does" statement, which tells what the function of the paragraph is. (Is it offering a definition, giving a reason, comparing or contrasting, or what?)

A big step toward developing students' critical reading skills is getting them to distinguish between what a passage says and how that passage functions as part of the total discourse. While *The Aims of Argument* does not ask students to go as far as Bruffee does in outlining the texts they read, you can see that we have asked them to say what a particular paragraph or group of paragraphs *does*.

Seeing how paragraphs work together to perform a particular function helps overcome the notion that each major part of an essay can be developed in one paragraph, something many students try to do as a result of learning somewhere along the line to write the "five-paragraph essay."

Working through Difficult Passages

Critical reading is aided by summarizing and paraphrasing, and for this reason, teachers may want to turn to the discussion of those skills as presented in Appendix A (pp. 627–630). For students needing more help, we offer the following suggestion, which has been effective in basic writing classes.

Select a brief but dense passage from a text the class has been assigned. An example could be a passage with multiple voices, metaphors, or allusions, such as Quindlen's sixth paragraph. Ask students to paraphrase it after reading the advice on difficult passages and on paraphrasing in Appendix A. Remind students not to leave out any of the ideas in the original version—this is not to be a summary.

In a subsequent class, project an overhead transparency of the original version. On the transparency, we use a different colored Vis-a-Vis pen to underline each essential idea. Below the original you might place several of the student paraphrases, which the class can compare to the original. For each idea underlined in the original, students should find the corresponding section in the student paraphrase. Discuss which paraphrases are the best grammatically and stylistically as well as which provide the most helpful interpretation of the original text. Here is an example of how we paraphrased the sixth paragraph of Quindlen's essay:

Original version:

Times are bad, and we blame the newcomers, whether it's 1835 or 1991. Had Morse had his way, half of me would still be in Italy; if some conservatives had their way today, most of the children at P.S. 20 would be, in that ugly phrase, back where they came from. So much for lifting a lamp beside the golden door.

Paraphrased version:

Just as nineteenth-century Americans blamed immigrants for crime and violence, so do many Americans today argue that immigrants are responsible for society's problems. The solution for people like Samuel Morse then and conservatives now is to shut the doors and keep out the poor, such as Quindlen's own Italian grandparents and the third graders she recently visited in Public School 20. But this solution contradicts the spirit of the Statue of Liberty, and the words written there inviting the hungry and poor of the world to come here to find a better life.

Teaching students to paraphrase carefully aids not only in their reading comprehension, but also in their ability to use indirect quotations accurately when they draw from source material as they write their own arguments. In those circumstances, students too often opt for extremes: either a direct quotation from the source, or a fleeting reference to it.

Identifying Reasons

While students generally have no trouble identifying the thesis or main claim in a well-written published argument, they are much less able to pick out the reasons that support it. You might say that they can't find the forest because of all the trees (background information, evidence, impressive facts and opinions in support of the reasons, rebuttals of opposing views, and so on.)

We suggest that after the class has read and worked through "Making the Mosaic," you work together through the reading process using some of the essays in Part Two. A good one for beginners is William Raspberry's "The Myth That Is Crippling Black America" in Chapter 15. Here, the second paragraph offers Raspberry's two reasons for claiming that black Americans should stop seeing racism as the main source of all their problems.

A Form for Considering Rhetorical Context

When we assign beginning students an argument to read on their own, we give them a prereading handout offering guidelines for considering rhetorical context such as the following.

Title of argument:

Topic of argument

Issues or questions that people debate regarding this topic:

Your current position if you have one:

Rhetorical context of the argument:

  Who wrote it:

  When it was published originally:

  Where it appeared:

Before reading, can you tell:

  To whom it is aimed:

  What author's purpose is:

ANSWERS TO FOLLOWING THROUGH EXERCISES

Page 17: Since this exercise asks students to draw upon their own prior knowledge, answers will vary considerably. The important thing is to generate a discussion from these notebook entries that shows students how much they can recall about the topic if they make an effort. Unless students have relatives who have immigrated recently, they may be unclear about our nation's current immigration policy. Instructors may wish to read up on it; the longer version of *Aims* contains a section of readings on immigration, beginning with a brief history of our nation's policies up to the 1965 Immigration and Nationality Act, which set our current policy.

Page 18: Immigration issues have not changed much since 1991, when Quindlen wrote this essay; mainly, new concerns have risen over the effects of welfare reform on legal immigrants. As states move to limit the services and entitlements of non-citizens, many legal immigrants, such as the elderly and disabled, have nowhere to turn. A liberal perspective in general endorses progressive social and economic policies that promote the rights and ensure the well-being of minorities and the poor. On immigration issues, a liberal perspective would argue for humanitarian policies such as family reunification rather than requiring immigrants to have advanced education and certainty of employment.

Page 19: Students should notice that Quindlen's first paragraph shows her preference for the mosaic rather than the melting-pot metaphor, clueing readers that her bias is for maintaining diversity rather than assimilation. The last paragraph, by defining the "true authentic American," shows that the essay will correct an opposing viewpoint of what a true American should be.

Page 24: A good paraphrase of Quindlen's fifth paragraph would be: A fear of strangers is not new to America. In 1835, Samuel Morse wrote a treatise entitled "Imminent Dangers to the Free Institutions of the United States through Foreign Immigration," in which he complained that the character of our nation was being "degraded" by the violence and rioting of the latest immigrant groups. Oddly, he included the Jesuits, a scholarly monastic order, among the troublemakers.

Page 26: We point out in the text the thesis, reasons, and major divisions of Quindlen's essay. Here are some other annotations that students might compare with their own:

About evidence in support of the reasons: Is the evidence in paragraphs five and six sufficient to convince readers that opponents of immigration in the nineteenth century were bigoted rather than wise? Has Quindlen given enough evidence throughout to convince her readers that the newest immigrants today pose no serious threat to our economy and social services? This is not the kind of essay that offers statistics and data, but what data would your students need to have in order to evaluate the position offered here?
About key terms: What do students think about Quindlen's definition of the "true authentic American"? How would they define American, in the sense of our national character? Is such a definition possible, given the diversity of our population today?
About assumptions that underlie the thesis and reasons: Quindlen is assuming that the latest immigrants will succeed, that is, they will pass through this life of poverty on the Lower East Side and go on to a more prosperous life just as generations of immigrants before them have done. Do you think she is correct in this assumption? Is she also assuming that the public schools such as the one she visited can do the job of educating these latest immigrant children for a life of success?
About opposing views: Do students want to know more about the gubernatorial candidate who is characterized here as opposing the current immigration policy? Is he or she really arguing for a policy that favors white Protestants? Do students think Quindlen is overstating the position or representing it fairly? How could research help them evaluate the essay on this point?

Bibliography

Bazerman, Charles. "A Relationship between Reading and Writing: The Conversational Model." *College English* 41 (1980): 656–61.

Brent, Doug. *Reading as Rhetorical Invention: Knowledge, Persuasion, and the Teaching of Research-Based Writing*. Urbana, IL: NCTE, 1992.

Bruffee, Kenneth. *A Short Course in Writing*. 4th ed. New York: HarperCollins, 1992.

Chapter 4
Teaching the Toulmin Method of Analysis

THE GOALS FOR CHAPTER 4

This chapter offers what we view as a supplement to the two chapters that precede and follow it. Chapter 3 presents a method for reading an argument critically; there we encourage a rhetorical and conversational approach to analyzing a text. Chapter 5 presents the art of inquiry, which teaches students to enter into a dialogue with the absent author of an argumentative text. This chapter on inquiry provides students with ten types of questions to pose and guides them in finding or inferring the answers. The two chapters offer a real and flexible way of evaluating arguments that is discursive and open-ended.

For teachers who want a more structured approach to analyzing arguments, we offer Chapter 4, in which we have simplified the model devised by Stephen Toulmin. Toulmin's approach to argumentation complements Chapters 3 and 5 (and even overlaps them) because it emphasizes not only thesis, reasons, and evidence, but also the social context in which an argument occurs: the attitudes, beliefs, and assumptions that people must hold in order to say that certain reasons are good.

Another advantage to the Toulmin model is that it can be diagrammed in a nonlinear form. For that reason, it helps students see an argument in its entirety, as if from above rather than within the text.

The most important thing to remember if you choose to use this chapter is that there is no point to applying the Toulmin model simply for its own sake. Finding the perfect fit between a particular printed argument (something real) and the diagram we offer in this chapter (something ideal) may not be possible or even desirable. The model is a tool that is useful if it helps readers think about elements of an argument that might not be immediately evident. Be sure to put the emphasis on getting the job done, not on preserving the tool.

SUGGESTIONS FOR TEACHING

The Diagram

Students sometimes try to fill in the boxes in the diagram on page 34 of the text. However, the space is really insufficient for them to do so, and it is probably just as well. They will need to create a slightly different version of the diagram for each argument they read or write. Also, the space for assessing whether a reason is "good" and "relevant" would have to be considerably larger. If we had had more space, we would have indicated that any particular piece of evidence should also be assessed in terms of whether it, too, is "good" and "relevant."

ANSWERS TO FOLLOWING THROUGH EXERCISES

Page 35: The text asks students to decide (1) if the second through fourth reasons in May's argument are good and (2) if these reasons are relevant. The following answers are not offered as absolute; questions of what is good and what is relevant are often open to interpretation and debate. We offer our views for you to compare with your own responses and those of your students. Make your students aware that there is no "right" answer; they should consider multiple views on the question.

Reason 2: Those close to the dying can come to terms with their impending loss through grieving in advance.

1. The reason sounds good because it appeals to our values of having sympathy for those who are bereaved. It does, however, put the relatives' well-being above that of the suffering patient, if we assume that the patient wants to die.

2. Students should see that relevance can sometimes be debated; that is, it is often a matter of perspective and interpretation. Here, for example, some students might say that the reason is relevant because if longer grieving in advance means a reduced sense of loss when the death occurs, then suicide would certainly shorten the length of the advanced grieving. On the other hand, some students might say that the suicide would not take place as soon as the patient received the terminal diagnosis. The patient would have to be suffering, and since the relatives would have had to witness some suffering, we could say that the suicide would not preclude the relatives' preparation for the death any more than it would preclude the opportunity for reconciliation. Also, some might argue that if the death is a planned event, the sense of closure and farewell may be more pronounced than if the patient had simply drifted away in semi-consciousness.

Reason 3: The community needs examples of patient, courageous people who "die with dignity."

1. Again, this reason appeals to solid values, in this case, our admiration for the human spirit that prevails over extreme adversity.

2. It is hard to call this reason relevant. The choice to go forward to meet death rather than wait for it is not necessarily cowardly and undignified.

Reason 4: The community needs the virtues of those who care for the sick and dying.

1. Is the reason good? Certainly, it is good to encourage in a society the virtues associated with caring for the sick and dying: love, selflessness, compassion.

2. Is the reason relevant? Some would say not, because many dying and chronically ill people will not choose the option of suicide, so the community will have ample opportunity to practice caring for the sick.

Page 36:   After students have read the student-written essay "Capital Punishment: Society's Self-Defense" (pp. 36–40), they could be asked to analyze it according to the Toulmin diagram. We offer our diagram on page 17. Other versions are possible.

A Toulmin Model for Analyzing Arguments

The Case: Capital Punishment: Society's Self-Defense
Claim: Capital punishment is necessary to protect society from serial killers

No qualifiers or exceptions given

Reason: If individuals can use deadly force in self-defense, society is also justified in using it, as in capital punishment.

Is this reason relevant? Only if the analogy holds up. Are the circumstances really similar? Individual is acting in panic and fear. Immediate threat of loss of life. No other options. So, *no*. Analogy is not strong.

Is this reason good? Yes, self-defense is valued; part of right to life.

Evidence: None, really. The author seems to see the analogy as self-evident.

Reason: Other methods of protecting society have proven to be ineffective.

Is this reason relevant? We would have to look at whether other methods really don't work, and if they don't, why they don't.

Is this reason good? Yes. Protection of general public is desirable.

Evidence: The long narrative about the Ted Bundy case.

Relevant? Yes

Good evidence? It's credible, but is one example really sufficient?

Reason: Our society does not see life as sacrosanct. "The preservation of life, any life, is not an absolute value that most people in this country hold."

Relevant? This is only relevant if we believe that taking the killer's life is the only way of removing the threat they pose to the public good.

Good? This is only as good as the motivation for taking a person's life in a given situation. Also, it bows to the will of the majority.

Evidence:

1. Declaration of Independence: All men endowed ... with unalienable rights. Here life is not more sacred than liberty.

Relevant? No, because founding fathers meant all the rights for each person. Not "my pursuit of happiness overrides someone else's right to life."

Good? A credible source.

2. Patrick Henry: "Give me liberty or give me death."

Relevant? Not at all. Henry was talking about choosing death for himself, not executing someone else.

Good? A credible source.

3. U.S. military sends soldiers to die to defend our freedom.

Relevant? These deaths are a sacrifice. It would be more relevant to speak of killing our enemies in the wars.

4. People protect their families with use of deadly forces.

Relevant? Yes.

Good? Only if we accept the earlier analogy in the first reason.

Refutation of Opposing Views

Objection: An innocent person could be executed.

Rebuttal: We would not ban automobiles in this country just because they pose a threat to innocent lives. Analogously— Like autos, capital punishment improves life for the society as a whole.

Relevant? The analogy does not hold up. The execution is not an accident in the same sense as an auto accident.

Objection: Capital punishment is cruel and unusual.

Rebuttal: The methods of capital punishment are less cruel than the acts committed by the serial killers. Many people in our society suffer pain, for example, as a result of illness.

Relevant? Not really. You would have to compare capital punishment with other punishments.

Bibliography

Toulmin, Steven, Richard Rieke, and Allan Janik. *An Introduction to Reasoning.* 2nd ed. New York: Macmillan, 1984.

Chapter 5
Teaching Inquiry

THE GOALS FOR CHAPTER 5

Inquiry is the aim of argument that provides a foundation not only for the other three aims in the text, but also, in the longer view, for students' participation in academic and civic arenas, in which claims to truth must be preceded by open-minded examination of their own and others' views. When we begin the chapter by saying that the end or purpose of inquiry is truth, we mean not an absolute truth, but a position that has withstood the challenges of our own and others' rigorous intellectual inquiry.

Seeing such exploration as a form of argument is a new experience for most students, who think of one who argues as either advocate or adversary. This chapter purposefully thwarts the common tendency of students to jump to closure on a position, and shows instead that one who argues can value the question over the answer.

More than any other chapter in the text, Chapter 5 reveals the book's debt to a view of rhetoric as hermeneutical, that is, as recognizing the complementary nature of rhetoric and interpretation, specifically, disinterested interpretation. What has been called "philosophical hermeneutics" is the search for "the unsettling question, not the settled interpretation" (Crusius 75). As they work through this chapter, students learn to question arguments in a way that opens up the issue at hand, revealing its complexities.

Uncertainty is not something that their past educational experiences have taught students to value. But our view of rhetoric makes uncertainty a necessary first step in preparing to write an argument. A rhetoric that is hermeneutical cultivates "the experienced or nondogmatic person, open to exchange with others and aware of . . . the situatedness of one's own views, not in eternal verities, but in the contingencies of time and circumstance . . ." (Crusius 59–60).

Since we began teaching inquiry as an aim of argument, students have increasingly reported to us a genuine change of mind on some issue, resulting from an enlarged perspective on opposing views or on a discovery of shortcomings in their own argument. Moreover, students enjoy posing unsettling questions and challenging each other's arguments in good faith. Many of them have never before discovered the pleasure of this active an intellectual engagement.

SUGGESTIONS FOR TEACHING

The Questions for Inquiry

This chapter presents a conversational method of analysis which is less structured and more open-ended than the Toulmin model in Chapter 4. Students like the idea of writing a dialogue; the genre invites creativity, and you will have to put up with the occasional interrogation that goes off on a tangent. However, if students keep returning to the ten Questions for Inquiry on pages 44 and 45 (and reprinted for convenience on the text's endpapers), they will find that these can best open up an argument for real inspection.

It helps to think of these ten questions as *topoi,* or places to look, with each "place" capable of generating numerous questions about a particular argument. Students should be able to say which one of the questions in the list generated a particular passage in their dialogue.

Inquiry into Written Arguments

Although we model the process of inquiring into a written text on pages 48–52, this type of interaction with a text is so novel to students that you really need to model it in class yourself before asking them to attempt it on their own. The best way is to assign another short argument and guide the class in creating a dialogue with its author. (One possibility might be student Amber Young's essay on capital punishment on pages 36–40.) The dialogue needs to be written out—on the chalkboard, on overhead transparencies, or on a projected computer screen or networked computers. (Students like being able to take away a printout.)

As you guide them in this collaborative effort, you need to stress:

1. The dialogue must begin with a question about the claim. Restating the claim can lead to a question from almost any other "place." With Young's essay, a question about definition would be a fruitful next step: Has she really specified which murderers should receive the death penalty?

2. To avoid a superficial conversation that does little more than restate the argument, students need to pursue a single line of questioning beyond the initial Q and A. For example, if students ask Amber Young why society is justified in using capital punishment, they can easily supply a response: that individuals may kill in self-defense. Digging deeper into the argument requires a follow-up question about that reason: Why is an individual's right to self-defense analogous to society's right to use the death penalty?

3. The most unsettling questions are those that don't have an obvious answer in the text of the argument. For example, Amber Young's argument becomes unsettled when we ask her to specify how using deadly force in a situation of self-defense is similar to using the death penalty.

4. Inferring an answer involves careful reading, interpretation, and a good-faith effort at role-playing, as students must step into the shoes of the writer, even if they incline to disagree with him or her. Here, they would have to try to help Young draw out the similarities between self-defense and the death penalty.

The process of writing a dialogue with a text allows students to practice a range of critical reading and thinking skills. They play the roles of both believers and doubters, to borrow Peter Elbow's terms. Using the Questions for Inquiry gives students a strategy for doubting; composing answers gives practice in careful reading, paraphrasing, and summarizing, but, more importantly, it makes students responsible for bringing the text to life based on their interpretation of the author's aim and argument.

An Analysis Based on Inquiry

In the text, we work through the process of writing an analytic essay based on inquiry, with two examples of such essays (pp. 54–56 and 58–59). We can add here only that this is a difficult assignment for many students. Teachers may want to omit this assignment, or return to it later, since inquiry carries through the other three aims.

While we warn against writing a summary in assigning the analytic essay, too often that is what students produce, especially if they are analyzing an argument they like or agree with. To avoid this, students need to look closely at how the two sample analytic essays are organized: What are the major subdivisions, and how are they introduced? We would also point out how terms from the Questions for Inquiry appear in the openings of paragraphs.

We suggest that you ask students to bring to conference both the draft versions of their analyses and the dialogues that they should have written first. The dialogue is often more analytical than the draft essay, and teachers will be able to point out ways to bring the critical thinking from the dialogue into greater play in the analysis.

Inquiring into a Range of Positions

Moving from analysis of a single text to synthesis of multiple texts, this section helps students with skills essential to researched argumentation. If students are to integrate multiple sources in developing their own arguments, they need strategies for comparing and organizing the source material, as well as critiquing it. The exploratory essay, whether you make it a formal paper or not, is a way of beginning to research. You may want to assign pages 610–626, on how to research an issue, and 626–637, on paraphrasing and summarizing.

While you may decide not to assign the exploratory essay as a major writing project, you will probably want to go over the suggestions on pages 59 and 60 and put them into application as prewriting for a researched argument with the aim of convincing or persuading.

Using Inquiry by Peers as Prewriting

Asking students to write a preliminary position statement and having their classmates probe into that position statement using the Questions for Inquiry is an excellent in-class exercise that helps students refine their thinking. You might have students question each other in small groups or in pairs. If they don't write out the dialogue, we suggest asking each student to follow up on the conversation by writing a journal entry or a "free-write" that sums up the chief challenges offered by peers and the rethinking that will have to result.

ANSWERS TO FOLLOWING THROUGH EXERCISES

Page 52:

1. a.   We would question Levin about the evidence he offers in paragraph 6, where he reports the results of an informal poll that he took. Would four people be a sufficient sample for drawing any real conclusions? Would these mothers have a fair and disinterested view? Isn't their reaction exactly why we don't put

relatives of a crime victim on the jury that tries the person charged with the crime? We would also ask Levin if he has any evidence showing that torture has ever saved innocent people's lives, as he claims.

b.   We would ask if Levin would advocate torture in the same sort of situation in which a preemptive attack would be used. For example, would he allow Nation A to torture one soldier from Nation B if doing so would save the lives of many civilians in Nation A?

Bibliography

Crusius, Timothy W. *A Teacher's Introduction to Philosophical Hermeneutics*. Urbana, IL: NCTE, 1991.

Chapter 6
Teaching Convincing

THE GOALS FOR CHAPTER 6

In this chapter students should come to understand the concept of case structure as diagrammed on page 75 and be able to apply it successfully in a given rhetorical context. Even the first of these goals is not as simple as a glance at the diagram might suggest. Many students, even those at the graduate level, have never consciously organized a piece of writing according to the principles of case structure. Too often, teachers of subjects other than writing, at the secondary level and beyond, are content with receiving loosely connected discussions, so long as they are factually and grammatically correct. For many students, seeing an essay as the development of one main point is a new experience.

The second goal carries case structure into real application. Recently, one of our colleagues who teaches literature and who expects argumentative writing from his students complained that too often his students seemed to have no reason for putting a particular point where they did. He made his comment in a discussion of what teaching "rhetoric" was all about. His students' problem was that while they may have understood thesis, reasons, and evidence, they did not understand rhetorical context. They did not know how to present the case in a way that would have impact on a reader.

SUGGESTIONS FOR TEACHING

Structure and Strategy

This section works through the argument on drug testing by Anne Marie O'Keefe as an example of a case that has been strategically fitted to the likely attitudes of readers of *Psychology Today* in the late 1980s. Our analysis is reasonably thorough (pp. 76–83). However, merely assigning these pages as out-of-class reading may not be enough to help students see the structure in the actual text of the argument. Some of our students only truly understand how case structure can shape an essay when they read the much simpler student-written essay at the end of the chapter. Therefore, we suggest that you work through O'Keefe's essay in class, asking students to identify what sections of the essay (by paragraph number) develop each reason outlined on page 77.

The Process of Convincing: Preparing a Brief

In this section (pp. 84–100) we take students through a prewriting process, demonstrating each step and asking them to "follow through" with various short writing assignments that precede the actual drafting of an argument to convince. At any stage of this process, students may discover that they need to go back and revise one of their earlier stages, making adjustments to later stages also necessary. Including time for research, these prewriting activities could easily take a full week of student work.

Working toward a Position. As we state on page 84 of the text, arriving at a position worth defending always involves inquiry and usually involves research. We prepare students to research a topic (of their choice or one that we assign) by covering the appropriate material in Appendix A (pages 610–637). As a class, we make a library visit, during which a librarian introduces students to the indexes and reference materials most helpful in exploring public affairs issues.

The Audience Profile. Occasionally, an assignment to write an argument will specify a real-world audience, for example, a member of Congress or a university administrator. Such an argument can even be sent as a letter or for publication in the campus newspaper. Usually, however, students will have to create a hypothetical audience for their arguments. Our experience has been that students have real difficulty thinking specifically about an audience. When assigned to write an audience profile, they have such a general readership in mind that they can think of nothing to say about it; they then tend to drift off after the first two or three sentences into a statement of their own position. The audience profile is important, so we give our students an opportunity to revise until they have a clear sense of who their readers are.

Refining a Thesis. Students should see that the focus and unity of an argument depends on a clear and direct thesis, or claim. When discussing thesis sentences, you might want to refer in class (where your guidance can help) to the material in Appendix B on expressing ideas forcefully and writing emphatic sentences with subordinate information, such as qualifiers, worked in as modifiers to the main clause. This advice appears on pages 663–668.

Analyzing the Thesis. Recognizing the key terms of their thesis sentences will enable students to see exactly what they must defend. However, it will also help them see what might go into the argument in addition to the reasons and evidence—for example, what definitions need to be clarified, what exceptions might need to be stated, and so on.

Finding Reasons.   We like to require students to find more reasons than they will actually use. Our purpose is to get them to think independently of their sources, which they may rely on too heavily. We assign the eight "sources of good reasons" on pages 91–94 as *topoi,* or places where they may find reasons. We ask them to invent a reason for as many of the "places" as they can. The first category, the audience's belief system, is so large as to include the other seven, but we like students to think consciously about how ideology influences rhetoric. (See James Berlin's provocative essay, "Rhetoric and Ideology in the Writing Class.")

Selecting and Ordering Reasons. Strategy is the concept to stress here. Students ought to be able to explain why, given their stated audience, they would emphasize a particular reason and why they would reject particular reasons.

Using Evidence. Just as with selecting reasons, students need to be aware of a skeptical audience and what evidence it is likely to find both good and convincing, as well as sufficient. We have found that in preparing their briefs, students often do not give enough thought to how they will support their reasons. It is a good idea to have each student exchange his or her audience profile and brief with a peer, and then question each other about the notes each has made regarding evidence.

From Brief to Draft to Final Version

Students may not require a full week to write a first draft if they have done a thorough job of working up their brief; however, they should have at least a weekend. We often cancel class and instead schedule conferences to review these early drafts, directing students to consider the suggestions listed on page 106. We then ask students to bring a revised and typed version of the draft to the next class meeting. Students exchange papers, using the Reader's Checklist for Revision on page 108 as a guide for commenting on each other's drafts. When students turn in their final version, we have them do so in a folder, which contains both earlier required versions. Students get credit for the drafts and for the peer editing work.

A Note about Plagiarism

Using this process approach to writing arguments almost guarantees that students will have to be involved in thinking through and working out an original argument, tailored to a specific audience. We insist on seeing the drafts, and in seeing that global changes have occurred, where necessary, rather than just cosmetic clean-ups. We have not had a problem with plagiarized or canned essays since we have begun using this approach.

ANSWERS TO FOLLOWING THROUGH EXERCISE

Page 84:

1. O'Keefe's essay is very tightly organized because the three major subdivisions of the case are outlined in the list of questions with which she ends her introduction. The first three group together around one issue: Why is there so much drug testing now? The opening words of paragraphs 3 and 4 refer to this group of questions, while the opening sentence of paragraph 5 clearly turns to the second main issue raised in the introduction: Are the tests effective? Her final question, about the costs with respect to workers' rights, is clearly raised in the opening words of paragraph 10 and again in paragraph 11. You should point out to students how deliberate repetitions of key words (or their synonyms) serve as direction markers for readers, making the progress of the argument clear and easy to follow.

Bibliography

Berlin, James A. "Rhetoric and Ideology in the Writing Class." *College English* 50: 477–94. 1988.

Perelman, Chaim, and L. Olbrechts-Tyteca. *The New Rhetoric: A Treatise on Argumentation.* Trans. John Wilkinson and Purcell Weaver. Notre Dame: U of Notre Dame P, 1969.

Chapter 7
Teaching Persuasion

THE GOALS FOR CHAPTER 7

We decided to treat convincing and persuading as separate aims because we believe that people often argue simply to earn other people's assent, while at other times they want a much stronger response. To this end, writers go beyond making a logical and well-researched case. To motivate others to cast a ballot, buy a product, join an organization—to *act* in some way—the arguer generally calls on skills that the public refers to as "rhetorical." One of our goals in this chapter is to get students to see that these rhetorical skills can be used ethically and responsibly, in ways that promote understanding and consensus—not just in the superficial ways suggested by the image of the "read-my-lips" politician.

We have another goal in teaching persuasion, despite the suspicion with which it is viewed by the general public as well as many of our colleagues. Convincing, as it is generally practiced, is often deficient in self-awareness. Those who argue within the conventions and expectations of convincing typically believe in some version of "pure reason." They see themselves as engaging in rational discourse and as appealing to what Chaim Perelman calls the "universal audience," or all reasonable people.

Our chapter on convincing goes some distance toward revealing the fiction of this position; we have shown that when we argue well we also create an impression of our own character and competence (the appeal to *ethos*), which plays no small role in winning the adherence of our audience. And all arguments either invoke or assume values that claim us emotionally as well as intellectually, so that *pathos* is never truly absent either. Persuasion, then, is present but submerged in convincing. Treating persuasion as a separate aim, however, brings it into full light and focus. Students should learn that an argument is situated in human contingencies.

More specifically this chapter aims to make students aware of, and competent in using, the rhetorical skills essential to persuasion: ethical appeal, emotional appeal, and the appeal of language that is carefully chosen and arranged. We have found that our model of these skills, Martin Luther King's "Letter from Birmingham Jail," inspires rather than intimidates our students. It is a *tour de force,* but the combination of ethical purpose and rhetorical skills makes it just the example we sought. Students will recognize in other persuasive prose the techniques King uses.

This chapter concludes with a brief section on visual forms of persuasion. We include visual persuasion mainly to complement our discussion of verbal persuasion and give students an opportunity to review and apply some of the concepts they have learned. We think the inclusion shows how cultural context conditions "readings" of the visual texts. Interesting discussions of the rhetoric of news photography and advertising images are found in the two essays by Roland Barthes which are listed in the bibliography for this chapter.

SUGGESTIONS FOR TEACHING

Analyzing Your Readers

The three sets of questions on pages 114–116 are difficult ones to answer. Students need to read King's letter and our discussion of his audience analysis before they attempt to analyze an audience for a persuasive argument of their own. Students need to see that audience analysis for persuasion is considerably more thorough than the short audience profile we described in Chapter 6. Rather than assigning a paragraph, as we suggest for the convincing essay, it is better to have students write responses in list form to as many of the questions about audience as they can in each of the three categories.

Teaching "Letter from Birmingham Jail"

King's "Letter" is long, and students need to read it carefully to appreciate it. We suggest that you spend some time in class prior to assigning it, going over the background provided on pages 116–118, supplementing it if you like. Then, have students simply read the "Letter" for a homework assignment. Remind them that each reading after their first will add to their appreciation of King's skills as a rhetorician. You might also ask that they respond to this question in their writers' notebooks: What did you notice as particularly effective? It is a good idea to have students notice things for themselves before they start reading our analysis (pp. 131–140), which ought to be a separate assignment.

Drafting a Persuasive Essay

Here we take students through the prewriting and drafting steps that they completed for their argument to convince, but with specific exercises to direct students' attention to the appeals of character, emotion, and style. If students are selecting their own topics for this assignment, you really need to intervene, guiding them toward topics that warrant persuasion. Ask students what they are trying to motivate their readers to do. Some successful combinations of audiences and topics for persuasion in our classes have included persuading smokers to conform to smoking restrictions; persuading abortion protestors to volunteer in ways that will improve the lives of babies born to poor or drug-addicted young women; persuading school teachers to design tests that allow for learning differences; and persuading teens with substance-abuse problems to seek help.

As with the writing assignment for convincing, we suggest that you allow at least two weeks for the entire project, with in-class work on prewriting, first-draft conferences, and peer exchange of revised drafts. Alternatively or additionally, it is helpful to ask one or two students to share their drafts with the entire class, either on photocopies or overhead projection, with everyone contributing to a discussion based on the questions for revision on pages 148–149.

The Appeals of Persuasion in Visual Arguments

We want the material on visual persuasion to reinforce what students have learned about reading and writing verbal arguments. To that end you should stress that, as with reading a written text critically, any "reading" of a visual text depends upon the context in which it is viewed and the viewer's prior knowledge of the subject addressed by the argument. (Editorial cartoons, addressing a particular occasion or issue, age especially quickly.) You might ask students to consider how the questions about rhetorical context on page 17 of the text can be applied to visual arguments. Students need to recognize that certain features of a visual argument may be persuasive to some audiences but not to others: A viewer reads significance into an image based upon his or her own social and cultural background and setting. You might emphasize this point when you discuss the Silver Jeans ad, which conveyed no message about race relations to Canadian viewers, among whom interracial dating does not attract notice.

You might want to have students find visual arguments on their own or create them, if they are so inclined.

ANSWERS TO FOLLOWING THROUGH EXERCISES

Pages 133–134:

1. In paragraph 2, King offers as a reason his professional position with the SCLC, which had a Birmingham affiliate that requested his presence. His description of the SCLC's work should appeal to religious leaders. In paragraph 3, King offers a more personal reason—his own crusade against injustice, which he supports by comparing himself to Hebrew prophets and the Christian apostle Paul. In paragraph 4, he reasons that as an American citizen, it is his responsibility and his right to fight injustice in any community in our nation. This argument should appeal to ministers who see a connection between religion and responsible citizenship.

2. King argues that one has a "moral responsibility to disobey unjust laws" (paragraph 15). This reason obligates King to define just and unjust laws. His first definition, that a just law squares with the law of God (paragraph 16), assumes that such a law exists and that human beings can have knowledge of it. However, he strengthens this part of his case by using theologians' arguments to show that segregation laws would violate a higher moral order condemning separation. His second definition (paragraphs 17–19) is based on the more secular concept of democratic equality, and he supports it with examples of laws denying black people their civil rights. Beyond definition, King also supports his reason through biblical and historical examples of civil disobedience (paragraphs 21 and 22), which his audience should admire.

3. In paragraphs 27–30, King responds that nonviolent resistance is not extremism, but a middle road between do-nothingness and violence. In paragraph 31, he shows that the label "extremist" has been applied to biblical and historical figures who would not compromise or retreat from their principles.

Page 135:

1. In addition to the opening and closing of King's letter, where we have already pointed out his efforts at identification, students might point to paragraph 14, where King speaks about his daughter's tears and his son's questions, an appeal to the common experience of parenthood. Or they might refer to any number of

places in the letter where King refers to biblical and historical figures that his audience would also revere: Paragraphs 3, 21, 31 and 44 are examples. In the long passage in which King discusses his disappointment with the white Christian church, he plays up his own membership and stake in the church (paragraph 34). Throughout, he refers to the "brotherhood" of "children of God," which binds all humanity.

Page 140:

1. *Paragraph 6:* Students might note that the purpose of this paragraph is to document the first of the four basic steps of any nonviolent campaign. The style of the paragraph suits the purpose: King writes a series of brief, simple sentences (sentences having one main clause) that form a list of facts about injustice in Birmingham.

   Paragraph 8: Students should notice the metaphors in the opening sentence. (Students might notice that imagery of light and dark recurs throughout King's letter.) You could also point out how, in contrast to paragraph 6, this paragraph contains many long sentences, with modifying phrases that subordinate the less important points to the points that King wants to emphasize.

   Paragraph 23: Here King uses repetition of relative clauses (beginning with "who") to describe forcefully his view of the white moderate. The penultimate sentence also uses repetition in a graceful turn on the idea of understanding and misunderstanding.

   Paragraph 24: Students should note the metaphor comparing unjust laws to dams and social progress to flowing water. But the standout device here is the extended metaphor comparing injustice to a boil that must be uncovered and opened up.

   Paragraph 31: Repetition works here to make memorable King's list of other so-called extremists. Note that he establishes the pattern—a question beginning "Was not . . . ?" followed by a quotation—but at the fifth repetition the question becomes elliptical, so as to avoid monotony and wordiness.

   Paragraph 47: King begins a series of sentences with "They will be . . ." in listing his real heroes. Students might also note the play on the idea of sitting down and standing up in the long last sentence, with the former used literally and the latter metaphorically. They should also note the metaphor of wells "dug deep" that King uses to describe the work of our democracy's founders. King uses water imagery frequently, and students could follow this image through to other paragraphs.

Page 148:

1. Joey Shanks's argument is directed not to the outspoken majority, but to the quiet dissenters who prefer not to draw fire from more vocal students. Students might discuss the possible motives for these people to remain silent.

2. We devised this brief of Shanks's case:

    Claim: The individual in society must possess the courage and the confidence to challenge and oppose the majority if he or she feels it is necessary.

    Reason: The power of the majority can be dangerous.

    Evidence: A group of people may be less intelligent and wise than one person alone. (Sources: Tocqueville, Twain, Clark)

    Evidence: Morality is not determined by people in a particular time and place, but is universal. (Sources: Nagel, Aristotle, Socrates)

    Students might want to suggest other evidence to show that majorities have abused the power granted them by their numbers.

3. Students might suggest some rearrangement. Paragraph 10 seems out of place. Could it be worked into paragraph 6? The thesis could be placed more prominently; perhaps, with some transition added, it could be the point that paragraph 6 leads to. Shanks could also have made it clearer that his single reason is the fundamental reason for speaking out; he might also have rearranged his evidence, as the Persian Gulf material is not the strongest he has.

4. We think Shanks could do more to present himself as a role model for the students he is trying to reach. Although he is honest about his own reluctance to speak out on that day, he claims that he usually does "ramble on." He ought not to portray himself so dismissively but say more about how he feels when he has at least tried to get others to see some issue differently. We do like his opening with the common experience of sitting in an uncomfortable "poly-wood" chair. Also, Shanks refers to several philosophers, authors, and historical and public figures that his audience would want to identify with. Likewise, they would likely bond with him in dislike of David Duke. We think Shanks could have appealed to his and his audience's common identity as college students, arguing that they have a responsibility to contribute to their school's intellectual climate by participating in rational debate.

5. We think Shanks does a fine job of setting the scene, showing a rather boisterous classroom (taught, we might add, by a very bright graduate student who resisted imposing her views on the class). We would also note the metaphorical use of "uncomfortable position," a double entendre. We think he could have done more, however, to motivate the audience to speak out, maybe by showing the implications of letting the majority trample the ideas of others with a wrong idea of their own.

6. We have already pointed out the transitional problem between paragraphs 8 and 9. His example paragraphs about Twain and Clark also need smoother introductions, with some indication of the point they are there to serve. The coherence is not tight between paragraphs 5 and 6.

7. We like the style of paragraph 5. The repetition of "she" as an opening to each sentence keeps the reader focused very tightly on the Hispanic girl. The series of successively shorter sentences leads to Shanks's main point about her.

8. The writing shifts in tone from less formal when describing the rhetoric classroom to a more formal, academic tone when the case is presented. The shift is apparent even in the thesis sentence, which opens paragraph 6. Your students might debate whether this shift is appropriate.

9. We think it is clear what the author wants. Your students might debate the effectiveness of the argument as persuasion.

Page 154:

2. Obviously, the difference in audiences has to do with women's interest in attracting men. The Request ad appeals to women who dress to enhance their sexual appeal. Simply, it argues that wearing Request jeans will make a woman look sexy. It appeals to the audience's desire to look beautiful; stylistically, the photograph signifies sexuality through the model's hair, pose, and dress. The Lawman ad makes a more rational and openly stated case. It argues that women sacrifice their real selves in order to please men, who impose upon women their definition of physical beauty and sexuality. In support, it offers examples of artifices that women use to appeal to men. It draws upon the appeal of character, suggesting that Lawman shares with its audience the view that women should be valued for who they really are.

Page 156:

Students may want to research and discuss how the Vietnam Memorial stirred debate when its design was initially proposed and when it was dedicated in 1982. Americans had distinctively different readings of the Wall, with some saying that it disgraced the dead it was intended to honor because it is so subdued and nonrepresentational. Today, your students may have different readings as well, since the design deliberately allows ambiguity. We believe that the "argument" of the Wall is more emotional than logical. Visitors walk the length of the V-shaped memorial, whose walls get progressively deeper and taller as they move into the years when fatalities were at their highest, tapering off again in the panels representing the final years of the war. Visitors literally read the Wall, and its text is the names of the dead, grouped by year of death. Certainly, the Wall argues that we should not forget this tragic war and the individuals who died in duty to their country, but it invites contemplation about war itself, and the reasons for it. Students may want to discuss the emotional appeal of touching the Wall and seeing one's reflection in it, and the stylistic appeal of the low structure embedded in the earth.

Page 158:

The arguments are similar in that they both address the issue of violence at abortion clinics; each shows how protestors may be so zealous that they fail to see the tragedy of murder if they are pro-life, and of abortion itself if they are pro-choice. While students might discuss the shared reasoning that one life is as precious as the other, the visual appeal in both cartoons also invites more thorough analysis. Each makes strong emotional appeals through such details as McCloskey's decision to portray the fetus as a small angel against a black background. In Luckovich's cartoon, however, the fetus is not recognizable. The manner in which Luckovich depicts the doctor is startling, even ghoulish, and students should discuss their reactions.

Bibliography

Barthes, Roland. "The Photographic Message." *Image, Music, Text*. Trans. Stephen Heath. New York: Hill and Wang, 1977. 15–31.

_____. "The Rhetoric of the Image." *Image, Music, Text*. Trans. Stephen Heath. New York: Hill and Wang, 1977. 32–51.

Corbett, Edward P. J. *Classical Rhetoric for the Modern Student*. 3rd ed. New York: Oxford UP, 1990.

Griswold, Charles. "The Vietnam Veterans Memorial and the Washington Mall: Philosophical Thoughts on Political Iconography." *Critical Issues in Public Art: Content, Context, and Controversy*. Ed. Harriet F. Senie and Sally Webster. New York: HarperCollins, 1992. 71–100.

Chapter 8
Teaching Negotiation and Mediation

THE GOALS FOR CHAPTER 8

Written arguments to convince and persuade are monologues. However, students using our text should see that even monological arguments must make accommodations to opposing positions and perspectives. In fact, we show that the dialogue of inquiry is where all arguments should begin. The goal of inquiry is to find a position that serves not our own interests and prejudices, but some common good. Our treatment of argument, we believe, answers the complaint that the values of monological argumentation are incompatible with the more open-ended, collaborative, and exploratory approaches that are found in many composition classes today (Lamb 13).

Negotiation and mediation fit into our sequence of aims by bringing students full circle, back into the dialogical methods of arguing to inquire. Our goal in this chapter is to get students to see negotiation not as it is commonly perceived (competitive deal-making) but as it has been reconceived by experts in the field (collaborative problem-solving).

Our treatment of negotiation is based on what the Harvard Negotiation Project terms *principled negotiation,* which they distinguish from *positional negotiation,* the more traditional form of bargaining. Principled negotiation was popularized in the 1980s by Roger Fisher and William Ury's bestselling book, *Getting to Yes.* Fisher and Ury advise that focusing on positions (what each party demands) is less likely to resolve conflict than focusing on the underlying interests of the parties in conflict. Their methods for resolving conflict complement many of the current interests of rhetoric and composition: collaboration, interpretation, and an emphasis on personal, social, and political contexts.

Argument as negotiation asks students to practice many of the skills introduced as part of inquiring into positions (dialogue, analysis, synthesis) and to combine these with skills learned in convincing (case-making) and in persuading (understanding difference, identifying common ground).

SUGGESTIONS FOR TEACHING

The Process of Negotiation and Mediation

As we said in Chapter 1 of this manual, when we have taught this aim we have assigned a single topic for the entire class, mainly because we are still experimenting with ways of teaching negotiation and want to be able to intervene. You should decide first whether you want your students to *negotiate* or to *mediate.*

If you focus on negotiation, your students will have dialogues with one another, as suggested in the Following Through exercises on pages 171–178. Ideally, you and your students should find an issue that divides the class to the extent that there is genuine conflict. This could be an issue the class wrote about for their argument to convince or persuade. If you focus on mediation, your students will read the arguments of others and mediate among those opposing positions. A topic that has worked well for us is the controversy over teaching *Huckleberry Finn* to high school and middle school students.

Either way, we have modeled the process with the abortion issue. The essays by McConnell and Willis explore many of the political, ethical, and moral dimensions of the abortion rights issue—and are not easy reading. We suggest you spend some time in class setting up the rhetorical context of both essays and going over the paragraphs on page 162 that serve as headnotes for each. Willis's audience is very important to her argument, but students need help conceiving of it, since they think of the antiabortion movement as conservative, not liberal. It is well worth going over paragraphs 3 and 4 of Willis's essay in class so that students understand the position of the "left wing of the right-to-life movement." You might also want to remind students of the Catholic Church's position on birth control.

As we have said, negotiation and mediation are dialogues. The writing project for this chapter may not be a monological argument (such as the mediatory essay we model in the second half of the chapter), but rather it may be a portfolio that records the results of conversations your students have had—with each other, if negotiating, or with published texts, if mediating. Such a portfolio could have six sections, based on the Following Through exercises that take them through the process:

1. Making briefs (p. 177)

2. Listing facts they disagree on (p. 177)

3. Explaining their different interests in the matter (p. 178)

4. Defining the problem in terms of the key interests that must be addressed (p. 182)

5. Explaining what additional information could help resolve the conflict—and if it did, how so (p. 183)

6. Stating how the problem was resolved and identifying some principles upon which the resolution was based, if possible—or explaining why resolution seems impossible (p. 184)

The Mediatory Essay

Teachers who want a more traditional essay assignment for this chapter can have students write a mediatory essay, as modeled here by Roger Rosenblatt's essay. We particularly like Rosenblatt's description of his "solution" to the abortion wars as a "wider road" rather than a "middle road" because that parallels our view of negotiation and mediation generally, in that they help to overcome difference, building upon a larger sense of identity that can unite the parties in conflict. You could do a great deal with Rosenblatt's use of persuasive appeals, if you have the time.

ANSWERS TO FOLLOWING THROUGH EXERCISES

Page 178:

The two writers would agree that sex has become more casual since the 1960s. Neither offers statistics, but such statistics could be found, documenting the average age when women lose their virginity, the number of sexual partners they have, and so on. It might be interesting to present McConnell with some statistics suggesting when this "sexual revolution" began: Was it in the 1970s, after the *Roe v. Wade* decision, or in the 1960s, when birth control pills came into common use?

Both authors might need to know more about the statistics of abortion. McConnell mentions that there are hundreds of thousands of abortions performed each year. Students could find out the actual number and possibly the rate of repeat abortions. Willis might need to know if abortion is being used as a means of birth control for a significant number of women. Also, surveys of women who have had abortions could reveal whether most of them weighed the moral dimension or ignored it.

Page 183:

1. Since neither writer wants abortion to become illegal, students might consider what, if any, restrictions McConnell would recommend. She has not outlined specifically any legal changes she would like to see put into effect. (Students might also research any state restrictions either proposed or already in effect: parental and spousal consent requirements, counseling requirements, mandatory waiting periods, and so on. Some of these are irrelevant to McConnell's point about the shirking of parental responsibility, but some are not.) Would Willis be likely to accept any restrictions on the legal right to abortion? If not, what other position on abortion could help to meet McConnell's objection that abortion has become too common and casual?

Page 194 (top):

We believe Rosenblatt's introduction is effective as a way of drawing readers into the essay with specific portrayals depicting intolerance at both extremes of the abortion debate. Rosenblatt wants readers on both sides of the issue to disassociate themselves from these extremists. Students should contrast this opening with the conclusion of the essay. In the closing paragraphs, Rosenblatt offers his readers a common identity as Americans that stands in sharp contrast to the portraits in his introduction: Students should look at paragraph 44, in which Rosenblatt persuasively calls for a "renewed national pride based on good will."

We think students might note Rosenblatt's fairness in presenting both sides throughout the essay. In paragraphs 14 and 15, he sets the religious arguments against abortion in a historical context that makes them seem in keeping with American values rather than in the negative light of violating the separation of church and state. His treatment of the opposing sides' views on individualism (paragraphs 18–22) is also notably even-handed. Neither side is portrayed as distorting individualism; he simply shows how the concept is open to interpretation. Likewise, conservative and liberal views on sexuality are treated in a historical perspective that avoids judgment, or at least seems to judge with equal cynicism the attitudes of the Puritan middle class and the free-wheeling upper and lower classes. All in all, Rosenblatt attempts to understand the conflict as more than a simple pro-con issue, making it the subject of disinterested intellectual inquiry.

Students might also note that Rosenblatt places blame for the conflict on social science thinking, which he points out has negatively influenced both sides' positions (paragraphs 33–36).

Pages 194 (bottom) and 195:

For both of these exercises, we suggest you compare various student versions after analyzing the original passages to identify the separate essential points that must be covered in each paraphrase.

Page 196 (top):

Rosenblatt's discussion of sexuality recalls McConnell's concerns about abortion leading to irresponsible sexual behavior. Rosenblatt casts this as a middle-class reaction to the sexual revolution of the 1960s. Would his discussion cause her to rethink her assumption about abortion leading to a breakdown of values?

The main concern expressed by Willis that Rosenblatt addresses directly is her assumption that the abortion issue is a political one. His discussion of the social science perspective (especially in paragraphs 34 and 35) speaks directly to her argument that abortion is a women's rights issue.

Your students should also notice that Rosenblatt's discussion in paragraphs 19–24 shows an understanding of both McConnell's and Willis's interpretation of the principles of individualism. In paragraphs 19 and 24, he represents Willis's view, while paragraphs 20, 21, and 23 show McConnell's perspective.

Page 196 (bottom):

Rosenblatt addresses Willis's interest in keeping abortion legal and unrestricted by such things as parental consent or waiting periods. He also addresses McConnell's concern that American society is becoming less responsible. Rosenblatt sees the needed responsibility more in terms of community than in terms of the breakdown of the family, however. His solution would not be hindered by the RU486 pill, since it avoids the "rights" issue of when life begins, as well as the question of whose rights have priority.

Page 197 (top):

Rosenblatt is specific about the "permit" aspect of his solution: He would like Congress to pass a law legalizing abortion. He is less specific about the types of legislation he believes would have the effect of "discouraging" abortion; however, he lists sex education, help for unwanted babies, and social programs to help families stay together. Given the purpose of his essay, a detailed treatment of such legislation is not appropriate.

Page 197 (middle):

Skeptics might want to know whether sex education reduces the number of unwanted pregnancies and how social programs could improve morals. They might want to know the costs of such programs and who would pay for them.

Page 197 (bottom):

1. We feel Willis and McConnell might be brought closer together by Rosenblatt's mediatory essay. As he says in paragraph 42, his "permit-but-discourage" proposal meets both "a sense of social responsibility" (which is one of McConnell's real interests) and "the advocacy of individual rights" in the "realm of respect for private values" (which is Willis's interest). His proposal is unlikely to satisfy McConnell's complaint that the sexual revolution has brought on the exploitation of women through uncommitted sex.

Page 199:

Philip Harvey's letter introduces a new issue not explicitly stated by Willis, McConnell, or Rosenblatt: that lifestyle contributes to one's political viewpoint and that women who see themselves primarily as mothers will find free access to abortion threatening to their values. Is it possible that Harvey's point could apply to McConnell and her position on abortion?

We included Anita Janda's letter because we thought her analogy was worth analyzing. It has a certain ethical appeal. But is enslaving a human being the same as aborting a fetus, and are both motivated by the desire to "assure [one's] quality of life"?

Richard Kelly's letter introduces the important point that Rosenblatt mentions in paragraph 21 of his essay: *Roe v. Wade* does not give "unqualified" access to abortion. Students should look at the wording of this decision, which is itself a kind of negotiated position.

Bibliography

Fisher, Roger, and William Ury. *Getting to Yes: Negotiating Agreement Without Giving In.* New York: Penguin, 1983.

Lamb, Catherine. "Beyond Argument in Feminist Composition." *College Composition and Communication 42* (Feb. 1991): 11–24.

Part Two: Readings: Issues and Arguments

Chapter 9
Answers to Questions: Environmentalism

Lame Deer and Erdoes,
"Talking to the Owls and Butterflies" (Pages 209–215)

1. The purpose of this question is to focus attention on technology. Of course, all human societies, including Native American cultures, depend on technology to some extent. But Western culture, in Lame Deer's view, has so totally separated people from nature that it is easy to forget our dependence on the biosphere: We have to make a conscious effort to "return to nature" on camping trips and other such excursions. He appeals to the natural and to a desire for wholeness, spiritual and physical. His argument is that we should respect the integrity of other beings, rather than manipulate them to fit our own desires.

2. *Genesis,* especially Chapter Two, is about power, about ruling and ordering. The biblical God is not "nature" but rather the maker and ruler of all creation. Human beings are subject to God's dominion, but they also rule over their own sphere, as symbolized in Adam's naming the animals. Lame Deer's Great Spirit is as vitally connected with his people as Yahweh was to the ancient Jews, but this god is pantheistic, a pervasive spirit linking all beings together rather than a ruler making distinctions and establishing hierarchies. According to Lame Deer, our arrogance derives in part from imagining ourselves as a special creation, "higher," closer to God than other creatures.

3. Lame Deer's point is that members of his culture recognize a deeply spiritual connection with all life so that, even when killing for food, they respect their prey as a part of the all-encompassing whole. The desacralized, objectified, contemporary world, however, lacks this sense of connectedness and fear of disturbing the order of things. The large-scale slaughters Lame Deer refers to in paragraph 13 are evidence of this.

4. The main purpose of this question is to encourage students to examine their attitudes toward magic and ritual. The tendency in Native American culture is toward unity and integration, toward a collective identity rather than individualism, toward a sense of the human being as part of all being. Technological society's outlook is fragmented, separating religion from social identity and dissociating spiritual healing from technologized medicine. As measured by treatment of specific disease and injury, modern, scientific medicine is spectacularly successful: but missing from it is the psychic, holistic dimensions of magic and ritual.

5. There can be no question that concern for the environment occupies the national consciousness and our political landscape more than it did thirty years ago. But are we moving closer to nature? Or are we caught up more than ever in the

power of technology to manipulate the environment, looking for technological solutions to environmental problems technology itself has created? It is difficult to argue that we are moving closer to nature, although we may be gaining a greater reverence for nature that could result in less environmental degradation.

Union of Concerned Scientists, "World Scientists' Warning to Humanity" (Pages 216–220)

1. Uncertainty is exploited as a reason to delay environmental action, especially by business interests and politicians who place economic growth above environmental concerns. A good example is the controversy over global warming. On the other hand, many environmental problems—loss of species, for example—are beyond dispute. Lack of certainty makes developing a coherent, overall environmental strategy difficult, but, of course, we will never know everything we need to know about anything we decide to do.

2. In a word, the problem as the scientists see it is growth—in population and in economic competition for resources. The earth is finite, while human demands are virtually infinite. Part of the problem is also inequity: relative prosperity in the West, grinding poverty almost everywhere else. It seems to us that the analysis of cause hits the main sources well. Neglected, however, is the contribution of science itself, not only in developing technology that damages the environment, but also in fostering an "intervene-and-manipulate" attitude toward all problems.

3. We need, the scientists say, to reduce Western overconsumption, reduce poverty world-wide, and minimize violence and war. Their "big-picture" view is impressive and praiseworthy; they see the interconnection of social and political problems with the environment. But they do not acknowledge, for instance, that part of the problem is the capitalist rationale of human effort. They speak of a new ethic but leave its content vague. And the sense they create that we must solve all major world problems to do something about the environment may actually discourage immediate, local effort by making all effort seem overwhelmed by the sheer magnitude of the problem.

Postrel, "The Environmental Movement: A Skeptical View" (Pages 221–229)

1. "Ideologies are messy"—that is, their tenets can be contradictory and fraught with tensions. Consequently, adherents to the "same" ideology can disagree rather sharply among themselves. This is a very important point that ought to be emphasized in any discussion of ideology. Postrel claims that the central value of environmentalism is stasis, or "steady state" conditions, where economic growth is halted or severely restrained. This claim seems to be contradicted both by radical ecologists, who advocate a return to earlier human conditions, and by most mainstream ecologists, who advocate economic growth

in the context of environmental responsibility. Some environmental advocacy is quite dynamic. We would call her characterization both inaccurate and unfair.

2. Postrel's ideology seems close to classical, laissez-faire capitalism, with its emphasis on individual initiative and distrust of centralized planning and governmental control. "Growth" to her means primarily technical innovation, a value certain to appeal to the audience of *Chemtech*. Of course, a key question remains: Can technology solve problems, such as environmental degradation, that technology itself is mainly responsible for creating?

3. There is clearly something to Postrel's account: We cling to technologies that create our complicated, hectic, and perhaps overly sophisticated lifestyle, but we also complain about and dream of escaping from that lifestyle. Lame Deer's appeal to spiritual values seems neglected in Postrel's account, as does his acute awareness of the need for a sense of community, or collective identity, to make human life meaningful. The nostalgia for a return to simplicity is only part of the appeal of green ideology.

Hynes, "Beyond Global Housekeeping" (Pages 230–234)

1. The analogy between women's traditional role in the home and their role in the environmental movement seems to us intuitively valid. But it is also true that some women are leaders in organizations with real environmental clout and that men sometimes play the global housekeeping role (in the Exxon Valdez cleanup, for instance, or the effort to cap sabotaged oil wells after the war in the Persian Gulf). Clearly Hynes wants women to play more than the traditional supportive role and seize positions of public authority and power. As she sees it, sexism has prevented a more forceful, visible role for women.

2. Her evidence and reasoning will not withstand careful examination: Her allegations amount to little more than guilt by association. Paradoxically, magazines like *Penthouse* and *Playboy,* which unquestionably exploit women, often act as agents on behalf of both feminist and ecological causes. The picture she sketches is far too simplistic. Her larger point—that women must take a greater role in the politics of environmentalism—is a serious one, but her argument here is unlikely to convince anyone not already sharing her point of view.

3. As Hynes employs the term, "environmental justice" means not only not exploiting nature for industrial resources, but also not exploiting the poor and allotting women power equal to men. In other words, solving our environmental problems requires thinking of the environment in the most comprehensive sense—a very important point, since social exploitation has so much to do with environmental degradation. Her proposals are basically mainstream, not anti-technology or "green" in the sense of returning to nature.

Collard, "The Environment: Us versus It?" (Pages 235–241)

1. Collard recognizes that environmental problems have complex sources—political exploitation, for instance, and dependence on polluting technologies, such as the automobile. But as the title of his essay suggests, he sees either/or thinking as the source of the problem, a view which omits much that the world scientists warn against: excessive population growth, exploitation of the third world, overconsumption by wealthy nations, exploitation of women. We find "Warning to Humanity" more persuasive because it has a more comprehensive viewpoint, but Collard's attack on simplistic thinking must figure in any workable solutions to ecological problems.

2. If one lives in a large city where mass transportation is relatively good, Collard's proposal to end our attraction to cars may sound feasible; elsewhere it is less likely. Nor does operating a car necessarily mean pollution and dependency on foreign oil: In the United States, for example, we could run cars on natural gas, which we have in abundance and which is relatively clean. Mass transit is only part of the answer and mainly for metropolitan areas. Special interests—automobile makers, oil companies, and the like—clearly do have a major role in maintaining the status quo, but cars also have deeply symbolic meaning for many people as a source of mobility, freedom, and social status.

3. It is hard, of course, to know which side is right: the view of Postrel and Collard that our ecological problem is manageable with minimal adjustment of the current economic order or the view of Lame Deer and the world scientists that, unless we drastically change how we live and how we think, we are headed for self-destruction or a life not worth living. It seems to us that Collard does underestimate the problem and that talk of crisis is warranted by world-wide conditions. At the same time, "us vs. it" is not likely to result in practical effort.

Cartoon by Guy Badeaux (Page 242)

This cartoon argues that people think about the earth in the same way that they think about consuming food, forgetting that earth and apple are not analogous. Students might discuss the emotional connotations of the visual image.

Chapter 10
Answers to Questions: Poverty and Welfare

O' Hare, "A New Look at Poverty in America"(Pages 246–259)

1. Perhaps the most surprising statistic for most people is the "in and out" effect; because the middle class tends to identify "the poor" with the underclass, we typically aren't aware that people go on and off the welfare rolls in large numbers. Most Anglo students also think the poor are mostly minorities, which, of course, is not the case.

2. Some of the most important facts about the poor are the following: the sheer number of poor people (40 million); the high rate of poverty among children (more than 20%); the high percentage of working poor (about 50% of all poor adults); the relatively low percentage of the federal budget devoted to the poor (14%); and the low percentage of income provided to poor people by welfare (25%). These facts suggest that a greater percentage of the budget needs to go to the poor, especially families with working adults.

3. O'Hare distinguishes, for example, between the "deserving poor," those too young or too old to work, and the rest of the poor, whom society expects to work. Another important category is the working poor—those who can and do work, but whose earnings fall below poverty lines. Finally, we have the nonworking poor, many of whom claim to be ill or disabled or for other reasons unable to work. Clearly the first group must receive adequate public assistance, since they are in no position to "help themselves." The same must be said for the truly ill or disabled. The challenge comes in helping those who work but remain in poverty and those able to work who don't. It is difficult to say what policies would prove both effective and politically viable. But it is probably true that whatever we do to assist the working poor will not help those not part of the work force and vice versa.

4. O'Hare focuses attention on the need for better day care, certainly of major importance in improving the conditions of poor children and their parents. Much more will need to be done: better prenatal care, better nutrition, improvement of schools, etc. Probably the chief barrier to helping poor children is that the middle class sympathizes with poor children more than their parents. But how can we assist the children and not the parents?

Photograph by Bruce Young (Page 260)

Students' own backgrounds and their contact with homeless people will influence their reading of this photograph. You might talk about how the setting—the nation's capitol—adds its own measure of meaning to the image. The blanket of snow makes the people's human forms almost indistinguishable: How do students react to this fact? Students might discuss whether the photo carries a particular political message, or whether it can be interpreted in a number of ways.

Marin, "Virginia's Trap" (Pages 261–270)

1. Marin creates sympathy for Virginia in many ways, all worth studying as models for student writing. Among his tactics are his description of her appearance and manner (paragraph 7), the invocation of her dignity (paragraph 8), the detailed factual description of her economic situation (paragraphs 10–13), the story of the break-up of her family (paragraph 20), the description of her enduring sense of loss after the death of her mother (paragraph 30). All of these are powerful appeals to emotion and break through the comfortable abstractions many readers use to think about poor people, especially minorities. Given what Virginia is and the world she knows, escape from cyclical homelessness seems almost impossible.

2. Clearly the following changes in policy might help: no deductions in welfare from money earned working until one's income exceeds poverty level, and then graduated deductions; public housing that is truly integrated into the community, not restricted to ghettos; and aid for dependent children indexed to poverty level rather than the presence or absence of men. A valid criticism of current welfare policies is that they do little to help recipients escape dependence on welfare. Marin shows us something of how the system works, without simply blaming government programs for cyclical homelessness.

3. The family arrangements described can be considered a "breakdown" only in that they do not conform to traditional middle-class notions of family, notions that today often do not even apply to the middle class itself. Note that Marin affirms the traditional family by telling us that the children would prefer "one permanent father." He is nonetheless aware that no universal standard can be invoked. He is trying to avoid being a "naive anthropologist," the student of alien cultures who sees only through the prejudgments of his or her own culture.

4. This is a very difficult question that may go close to the heart of the kind of homelessness Marin writes about. His analogy with Native Americans is worth exploring. Above all, as students delve into this question, an effort must be made to be wary of class bias and the temptation to substitute cultural for racial prejudice. Since the dominant norms in America are white, middle-class norms, it must be the case that Virginia's culture interferes with improving her life in a host of ways, major and minor. But does this mean that she must reject her culture? If so, how could she?

5. Marin sets up an effective rhythm, alternating between the kind of narrative possible only to someone with first-hand experience and the kind of analysis possible only to an intelligent, well-educated person. The "story" of Virginia's life is interrupted with an analytical passage (paragraphs 27–40) which puts this particular case into a larger framework; then Marin ends the essay by returning to Virginia's story. This organizational strategy helps Marin and his readers connect concrete experience with abstract explanation, one of the keys to

dealing with any significant social problem. Whether one agrees with Marin's assessments or not, the organizational approach is worth emulating.

6. Marin's style is good to look at closely because it is skillful and varied, but not so good as to be far beyond the capacities of a talented student. For example, center attention on paragraph 39—its sentence structure, word choice, use of repetition, and contrast—or paragraph 39, which uses many of the same devices for different effects. Connect the devices with emotional appeal. Contrast these paragraphs with less striking passages, such as paragraphs 10–13.

Lovern, "Confessions of a Welfare Mom"   (Pages 271–277)

1. The stages Lovern goes through might be described as follows: the anti-welfare, I-will-support-myself phase, which ends when she realizes she can't make enough; the "breakthrough"phase, when her friend leads her to see that she can get an education if she goes on public assistance; the putting-the-pieces-together phase, when her welfare, work, child support, etc. come together to make her condition satisfactory; and the final success phase, when she completes her degree and becomes self-supporting. In phase one she learns that her inherited attitudes toward the poor and welfare are not appropriate; in the second, that public assistance, though slow and perhaps in some ways not adequate, can enable single parents to gain ground; in the third, that "working the system" doesn't necessarily entail loss of values or self-respect; and in the fourth that welfare needn't become, as we are sometimes led to believe, a way of life. Lovern's experience, however, shows that the system probably works best for middle-class people, those most able to deal with the system and eventually overcome poverty.

2. To remain eligible, Lovern had to be in job training or working, but she as yet lacked the day-care assistance that would enable her to do one or the other. The problem here, which is similar to Virginia's, is the "all or nothing"mentality of current welfare policy. At the very least, the "disregards"for welfare recipients must be more generous, allowing them to earn more without losing benefits.

3. Health coverage was the chief barrier to going off welfare—Lovern had it on welfare, but would lose it if she went off AFDC, as she would also have to pay for child care. Here we see clearly the interaction between welfare and other areas of national policy. If we want to get people off welfare faster and permanently, we'll have to reform health and child care.

4. Perhaps there may have been alternatives for Lovern, such as appealing for parental help and/or more pressure on her ex-husband for support, but on the whole we would say she did the right thing—in fact, we think most Americans would strongly support welfare if it produced results as happy as this case. We

would go on welfare in her circumstances; certainly it makes better sense than spinning one's wheels in perpetual poverty, working but not being able to make a living.

Kallick, "A Post-Liberal Approach to Welfare" (Pages 278–284)

1. Kallick's four "red herrings" are the following:
    i.   Welfare is too expensive. (AFDC makes up only 1% of federal outlays, all welfare 12%.)
    ii. Welfare goes mostly to blacks. (Blacks and whites receive welfare in almost equal numbers, 39% of recipients being white, 37% black.)
    iii. Fraud is rampant. (It exists, but not as a large percentage of welfare claims, and most of it is small-time.)
    iv. Welfare recipients should get a job. (As Kallick points current economic policy requires a certain amount of unemployment.)
   We agree with Kallick that these four are nonissues, and think that O'Hare's study confirms his assertions. But we also think that social assistance as a whole (including entitlements) needs massive rethinking, a possibility he does not raise.

2. Kallick's five "genuine" issues are the following:
    i.   The "taking" of welfare is not complemented by "giving." In general, welfare is approached in negativistic terms.
    ii. The welfare bureaucracy is inefficient.
    iii. Our attitude toward the family needs to change, especially with regard to single-parent families headed by women.
    iv. Failure to pay child support needs to be addressed realistically and constructively.
    v.   We need to find ways to make being out of work more positive—time in which things are being gained rather than only lost.
   We certainly agree that the moralistic, punitive attitude toward welfare recipients is both anachronistic and unproductive. But we don't think, for example, that "deadbeat dads" are really central to the problem, and it seems to us that the depth of the poverty question is not sounded here.

3. A major addition to the first list should be the common misconception that immigrants, especially illegals, are straining social programs. With regard to the second, Kallick hits on a major point—that our economy requires large numbers of unemployed people and even larger numbers of working poor—without really drawing the conclusion such an insight almost entails: That if we must have unemployment and poorly paid workers, then our social programs must do more, much more. Clearly this neoliberal wants to avoid being labeled a socialist.

4. Kallick calls attention to a classic double-bind for women especially: Traditionalists want them to stay at home and attend to their children, whereas feminists and other progressives want them to turn away from exclusive devotion to the home. The reality is that many women, poor or not, must work, and work

to the home. The reality is that many women, poor or not, must work, and work at low wages, making "choice" a moot issue. For most contemporary Americans, work is not just the way one makes (or tries to make) a living—it is, rather, self-defining, integral to self-esteem. For this reason, we see no reason to imagine that attitudes toward work and family are likely to change. We had best work with current attitudes in the hope of improving conditions generally, rather than working to change attitudes that must evolve naturally, in their own good time.

Murray, "Keeping Priorities Straight on Welfare Reform" (Pages 285–289)

1. By "carrots drive out sticks" Murray means that providing incentives to do something is more effective than attempts to punish behavior we consider wrong or destructive. Presumably Murray would then favor policies that encourage people to marry and stay married—i.e., the traditional family. But since he articulates only a policy objective without saying how he would achieve it, we cannot know what carrots he would advocate.

2. One point that Murray makes is certainly worth pondering: that the experts are often wrong, that no amount of knowledge or study will be able to predict the outcome of a particular social policy. Experimentation, therefore, does seem justified. But what works in one state, even if we can agree that something has "worked" hardly guarantees success elsewhere, and turning the states loose to try virtually anything will certainly result in gross inequities. Of course, inequities already exist. On balance we think that well-informed, well-intentioned experimentation is needed, but that "wide latitude" can easily be too wide.

3. Yes, Murray is right. No politically feasible welfare policy can hope to do more than reduce the current level of collective suffering. But having said this, we don't believe that Murray's animus toward welfare is likely to reduce suffering if translated into policy, nor that, even if the traditional family could be restored, that this alone would go far toward alleviating poverty and its associated problems. A two-parent poor family is still poor.

Funiciello, "Ending Poverty as We Know It" (Pages 290–299)

1. By the principle of social security, Funiciello means that some people draw money from a common fund (mostly the retired in social security) while others pay into it (younger workers). The idea, of course, is that contributors now will be benefiting later. A guaranteed national income involves the principle of income redistribution, but many who draw will never contribute or contribute little to the common fund, which opponents will certainly point out. But, of course, the same objection applies to social security. If we approve of social

security, why not a guaranteed annual income? Is the question implicit in Funiciello's argument.

2. According to Funiciello, the chief advantages of a guaranteed national income would be the following:
    i.   It would simplify social assistance.
    ii. It would reduce bureaucracy.
    iii. It would pay for itself.
    iv. It would release the creative energies of the poor.

    If these alleged benefits did result, all would be appealing, especially the last. The alienation and hopelessness of the poor is a tragic waste of human potential. The major disadvantage would be that the poor would still not be integrated into the economy in a complete sense, and useful work is what most of the jobless poor claim to want.

3. A family trust fund would be the means by which the guaranteed national income is financed—by analogy to social security, whose "fund" is unfortunately now absorbed into general revenues. Such a fund could be created and sustained in many ways, Funiciello suggests, such as by earmarking a small percentage of FICA for it and increasing inheritance taxes. The idea would be to build long-term resources for family assistance with minimal strain on the middle class, whose support is essential for her proposal to work.

4. She proposes a voucher system that would allow relatively poor people to choose the social services they wish to use, on the premise that such a "market system" would eliminate or reduce programs not in high demand. In this way, she believes, the welfare system would reform itself, much as services and goods not wanted in the general economy simply are not produced. The fear, of course, is that such vouchers might not be used in the best way, as (for example) food stamps are now sold or traded illicitly for alcohol or other drugs. Trying to specify and control what the poor should want, however, may be a losing proposition in any case, and the paternalistic attitude connected with it may be a large part of the whole poverty problem.

5. Much "income redistribution" by one means or another benefits the "haves," the relatively well-off, which explains in large measure why so many resent any effort to improve the conditions of the poor. What goes to "them" can't go to "us." We think there is a large measure of truth to what Funiciello says, but such insight hardly alters the political realities. Many commentators fear that we are headed toward outright class warfare if attitudes and policies toward our poor don't change markedly and soon.

Chapter 11
Answers to Questions: Immigration

Kennedy, "Can We Still Afford to Be a Nation of Immigrants?" (Pages 304–316)

1. Paragraph 3 divides the discussion into past and present, asking two questions about both: What motivated/motivates mass migration? and What were/are the consequences for the United States?
    The essay then develops as follows:
    i.   Past forces: "The Pull of America," "The Push of Europe," paragraphs 4–16.
    ii.   Past results: "The Immigrants in America," paragraphs 17–26.
    iii. Present forces: "Today's Immigration," paragraphs 27–31.
    iv.   Present/future results: "What Does the Future Hold?" "The Reconquista," 32–47.
    Transitional phrases and summary paragraphs include the following: Paragraph 17, first sentence (announces shift from cause to consequence); Paragraph 25 (sums up past immigration); Paragraph 26 (one-sentence transitional paragraph announcing shift of focus to present immigration); Paragraph 32 (transitional *opening* paragraph for new subheading—compare with paragraph 40); and the last paragraph, which reminds the reader of the central theme, i.e., the usefulness of history for understanding what is happening or may happen.

2. Kennedy contends that population increases and the Industrial Revolution "pushed" much of the European migration to the United States. In paragraph 11 Kennedy confirms population growth by citing figures; in paragraph 12 he describes the displacements that industrialization caused. Perhaps the most surprising fact is that many—40%—of the early immigrants returned home, which is hardly consistent with the "land of opportunity" myth.

3. Paragraphs 29 and 30 document the push from Mexico: a population more than triple what it was in 1945; an economy growing at double the U.S. pace, displacement of the rural, agricultural population, and so on.

4. The three historical circumstances which permitted relatively easy assimilation of early immigrants were the following: the immigrants never exceeded 14.7% of the total U.S. population; a growing economy could absorb new workers; and the immigrant population was diverse and widely distributed. Today's immigrants constitute only 8.7% of the total population, far less than in 1910; without immigration a labor shortage might occur. What makes the current wave different is its cultural homogeneity, its proximity to place of origin (Mexico), and its concentration in one region (the southwest U.S.). Unlike previous immigrants, the present group may not readily assimilate and may challenge the dominant power structure. There is more potential for social and political unrest and a greater challenge to our collective powers of toleration.

5. We must think and act anew because the situation *is* different: never before have we had such a large group of immigrants from the same area, speaking the same

language, sharing the same culture and religion, and settling in one region of the country. Part of the process of accommodation must be educational: the "natives" must overcome prejudices against Hispanics and their culture. In the long run, greater social integration of the two cultures and peoples must also occur, a process that depends on economic growth and justice. The United States must do what it can to improve conditions in Mexico. Finally, Hispanics must continue to learn English voluntarily and "Americanize" more completely to enjoy the full benefits of life in the United States.

Brimelow, "Time to Rethink Immigration?" (Pages 317–326)

1. The range of allusion and reference is impressively wide: to, for example, the origins of place names in England, events distant in time (the Norman invasion), events recent in time (the disintegration of Yugoslavia), thinkers, theorists and poets, both well-known and relatively obscure (Wattenberg, Masefield, Kallen, Chickering, Shakespeare, etc.). Clearly Brimelow is well-educated, even erudite, which certainly helps with *ethos*, especially authoritativeness. But his persona is also in places too superior, even self-congratulatory, as in his discussion of "polity" (paragraph 19). To the extent that some Americans are awed by British wit and sophistication, his *ethos* may be effective, but we think outside of upper-middle and upper-class Anglos his self-projection will alienate too many readers.

2. Basically Brimelow invites us to assume the position he assumes as an insider in the power structure—above it all, immune to the struggle of most immigrants from the third world. To the extent that we feel or want to feel superior to ordinary mortals, we can laugh with him, enjoy his irony, and share his condescending attitude toward the "colored" masses in the "underworld" of American society. He is right to expose the superficiality of platitudes about immigration, but his arrogant tone encourages many readers to resist even his best insights.

3. If we take a genuinely "long view" of immigration, we must reckon with a highly probable hypothesis—the "out of Africa" theory, which sees our species (*homo sapiens sapiens*) as emerging about 100,000 years ago in Africa and gradually spreading all over the globe, in the process displacing other *Homo* species, who likewise originated in Africa. We are truly "brothers and sisters under the skin." Ethnic identity seems almost superficial as one's historical perspective lengthens, and no one can say, finally, who "the natives" are, but only who happened to immigrate first to a particular region. In any case, our species seems to be perpetual pilgrims.

4. The evidence is concentrated in paragraphs 25–31. He tries to establish that the ethnicity is English, British ways adapted to U.S. conditions. He cites authorities as support—among them, John Jay, Theodore Roosevelt, and Calvin Coolidge. It would be foolish and dangerous to ignore the power of ethnicity to bind people together: If blood is thicker than water, it is certainly thicker than ideas. But while nations in Europe have tended to form around ethnicities, the

United States, which was always pluralistic, did not—ironically, given Brimelow's viewpoint, we owe more to English ideas than we do to English ethnicity.

Chavez, "What to Do about Immigration" (Pages 327–338)

1. By "culture" Chavez seems to mean roughly traditional American values—that is, "optimism, ambition, and perseverance" (paragraph 56). For her, apparently, to share a culture is to share a set of values. So understood, culture has little to do with heredity or ethnicity, and everything to do with acculturation. But culture includes more than values, and much that has entered into American culture in general has ethnic origins and is sustained by ethnic identifications. Ethnicity and culture, then, cannot be easily detached from one another.

2. By "national identity" most conservatives mean the norms of Anglo, middle-class life, in theory open to everyone. In practice an emphasis on national identity has usually had strong racial and ethnic implications, which accounts for Chavez's warning. Her bias is clearly toward class rather than race or ethnicity, as her advocacy of skills and education-based standards for admission of new immigrants shows. Basically she favors people who are already middle or upper class or who can achieve such a status easily. Understood in this way, her proposals are reasonably consistent, and given the makeup of those wanting to immigrate now, would not favor our white, European majority. But it would undercut our traditional openness to the dispossessed. Moreover, do we want to define national identity as Chavez does?

3. Actually the 1965 Immigration and Nationality Act has accomplished its objective—to undo the heavy bias toward European immigrants. Some would say it has worked too well. But as often happens the "success" of the law has been the result of changes the legislators did not foresee—hence, the idea of "unintended consequences." All significant policy has unintended consequences. For example, Chavez's proposal to increase the presence of the border patrol may result in greater suffering for illegals and increased violation of civil rights for U.S. citizens—not the outcome Chavez wants.

4. We could answer this question in many ways and at great length. Let's consider just one area, language. It is necessary for an immigrant to learn English well enough for at least basic communication. It would be desirable—helpful for the immigrant—to become as fluent as possible and to reduce as much as possible his/her accent, especially accents of low prestige. But it would be optional, of no concern to most Americans, whether the immigrant continued to use the first language in appropriate circumstances.

Mills, "Lifeboat Ethics and Immigration Fears" (Pages 339–348)

1. The lifeboat metaphor implies that the ship—the third world—is sinking and that the Unites States is the only refuge for the world's "huddled masses." It also implies that there is little space left for new immigrants, whose desperate attempts to climb aboard may capsize the boat and drown everyone. Such thinking reduces ethics to drastic calculations for survival, making the situation seem much worse than it is. Actually immigrants constitute a relatively low percentage of the total U.S. population and contribute more to our economy than they take away in government services. The lifeboat metaphor is more than misleading—it is a scare tactic.

2. In paragraphs 16–26, Mills points to some of the changes since 1965 that make the immigration laws enacted then problematical now. We can reduce the immigration multiplier and the strain on SSI by new legislation. Other problems may be harder to solve. What can we do about women coming to the United States to have a baby so that the child (and through the child, the parents) can claim U.S. citizenship? Change our definition of citizen? Not permit pregnant women to cross our borders? No doubt the 1965 legislation is overdue for reform, but all immigration laws will be to some degree circumvented and exploited.

3. Basically Mills accuses Chavez of being callous to the American underclass, especially blacks, and unconcerned with exploitation of both legal and illegal immigrants. Chavez is vulnerable to both charges. But she could well respond by saying that liberal U.S. social policy has not done much to help the underclass and that many immigrants historically have had a hard go at first. What we see as exploitation the immigrant may see as a first real opportunity for a better life. Probably the most serious issue Mills raises is the current tendency, hardly restricted to Reagan conservatives, to give up on our underclass. See the O'Hare excerpt in the poverty and welfare readings.

4. Mills appears to understand the bind clearly, and wants to cope with it by modifying immigration policy and protecting traditional liberal social programs. In the current political climate, the first is probably doable, the second probably not and ineffectual at best. The greatest weakness in Mills's article is that he has no new ideas for improving the lot of our entrenched poor. Without new ideas, his criticism of the conservatives lacks real force, lending only unintended support to laissez-faire attitudes.

Photograph by David Maung (Page 349)

Students should discuss their own reactions to the photograph; we would ask them to consider the following details: the way the wall itself dominates the picture, its prison-like quality, the way it dwarfs the figure of the border patrol agent, and the agent's own militaristic appearance. Our interpretation suggests that the photographer sees the wall as more indicative of a police state than of a democratic state. At the same time, the photograph suggests that the wall may be an exercise in futility, since the border agent is still necessary, and it would appear that he himself could scale the wall.

The most obvious wall between nations that comes to mind is the former Iron Curtain, and that portion of it between East and West Berlin in particular. The effectiveness of that wall depended on a heavy military presence.

Silko, "The Border Patrol State"   (Pages 350–356)

1. The border patrolmen's anger is "weird" because it has no immediate cause or object; no doubt frustration explains their anger, both in attempting to do an impossible job and in being constrained by law from employing even harsher methods. Racial animosities play a role as well.

2. The evidence is anecdotal, but nevertheless powerful because of its concrete, "real people" nature. Despite some legal challenges, the "profile" approach is used widely by law enforcement at all levels and in all locales, not just near the border, which lends additional credibility to Silko's allegation. It is also likely that the Border Patrol has greater de facto leeway to set aside individual rights, since some of their detainees are not U.S. citizens and are stopped at night in relatively isolated places.

3. Given that current immigrants are about 80% Hispanic and Asian, immigration may well be now associated with people of color. Insofar as talk about immigration has racist or ethnocentric undertones, it cannot help but distort clear thinking. So, for example, "control our borders" may well mean "keep brown-skinned, Catholic, Spanish-speaking foreigners out," rather than expressing respect for the law or a desire to cope realistically with the problems of illegal immigration. Our own ethnocentric view of the United States almost guarantees that we will not see things as Silko does—in terms of the ties of Native American peoples which long predate European settlement or the establishment of current borders between nations.

4. The obvious difference between the Berlin Wall and any fence we may erect between Mexico and the United States is that the former was constructed to keep its citizens home while the latter is a futile effort to keep foreign nationals from immigrating illegally. One is a fencing in, the other a fencing out. But this difference may not be very significant in the final analysis: both are highly artificial, desperate efforts to alter what Silko sees as natural forces and most others see as powerful political and economic motives. In any case, the fence will fail as the Wall did, so long as the motives to immigrate remain as strong as they are. What is perhaps most discouraging is that we don't seem to learn either from our own mistakes or from history. We do the same stupid things over and over.

Chapter 12

Answers to Questions: Feminism

Ebeling, "The Failure of Feminism" (Pages 360–362)

1. It seems to us that Ebeling has selected certain events of her life to support her view that feminism helped men and hurt women, and that she has suppressed other events which might help explain her current financial situation. Your students will have no problem thinking of questions about her marriage(s), her career preparation, her apparent second child, and so forth. Library research could reveal median income for men, women, single mothers, and others—but even if such figures show women making less, the argument that feminism brought on the inequality would be hard to make. Other research might show that the gap between women's and men's incomes has narrowed since the 1970s.

2. Ebeling seems to be arguing to express her own dissatisfaction with feminism and with men. (As we suggest in Chapter 1 of the text, expressing oneself is a common aim of argument.) However, she could also be arguing to convince young women that motherhood means depending on men and "traditional" family roles.

3. Ebeling uses emotional appeal to elicit sympathy for herself and for other single mothers who are in middle age (or approaching it) and looking for a man. The details about the singles scene in the opening and closing paragraphs are effective. However, her own character is not one with which all readers are likely to identify. Ebeling seems interested in finding a man primarily for financial support, and she seems too ready to adopt the role of victim.

4. While biology dictates that the female sex carries the fetus, susceptible to all the medical problems that pregnancy and childbirth can bring, there is no reason men and women cannot share equally in the parenting responsibilities. Most will admit that social custom rather than biology casts women in the caregiver role.

Friedan, "The Half-Life of Reaction" (Pages 363–376)

1. As Friedan sees it, the first stage of feminism in the 1960s and 1970s was a reaction to the restricted role assigned women during the years after World War II. In the "happy housewife heroine" role, woman's place was in the home. Rejecting this role, too many women entered a half-life, according to Friedan, in which they denied themselves a family life and a life of intimacy with men.

2. In paragraphs 9 and 10, Friedan is establishing her character as distinct from the "anti-family" or "man-hating" feminists. She shows how she and other women fulfilled their roles as wives and mothers, even as they gave birth to the feminist movement. The quotations in paragraphs 13 and 14 are convincing

evidence of the excesses of later feminists. Paragraphs 23 and 24 sound like personal attacks, but this is the only passage in this excerpt that we think comes close to Faludi's charge.

3. Certainly, many women—more so than men—want to have children, and the desire of some is so great that if they are unable to conceive, they spare no expense or effort on fertility treatment and other medical technology. What students might debate is the extent to which society has conditioned women to see childlessness as a tragedy. In our view, having children should obligate both sexes to assume the responsibilities of caring for them.

4. Students should paraphrase the second half of paragraph 21.

5. We see this excerpt from Friedan's *The Second Stage* as an attempt to keep feminism viable during the conservative decade of the 1980s. Rather than a part of what Susan Faludi has called the "backlash" against feminism, Friedan's book seems more a defense against that backlash. The social changes she proposes include new definitions of family and of full-time work that would satisfy the interests of women who want families but not compromise women's equality.

Quindlen, "Mother's Choice" (Pages 377–379)

1. Quindlen first describes the "cage" of motherhood as a thing of the past, supposedly made irrelevant by advances in birth control and the changed idea of women's role in society. Then she uses the details in paragraph 4 to suggest that a life unencumbered by children is a superficial one.

2. Her reasons are that motherhood is more fun and personally rewarding than "work." She is assuming that people pursue careers primarily for egotistical and material reasons, rather than because a career is fulfilling in itself. It seems a subjective judgment.

3. Because she chose to stay home with her children, she does not see doing so as a cage. She describes the experience in humorous ways; she acknowledges the grungy parts of the job, but in a way that makes us laugh.

4. Students might compare Quindlen's argument with the paragraphs in Friedan's essay (36 and 37) in which Friedan argues that for financial reasons, staying home is not a realistic choice for most women today. Does Quindlen bring up her own financial situation? Does she mention a husband? Does she mention her career? Students might also compare her argument with Kay Ebeling's.

Faludi, "The Backlash against Feminism" (Pages 380–394)

1. We find Faludi's evidence on this point convincing; she has a considerable number of sources, all well-documented.

2. Faludi means that men overreact when they interpret advances in women's social, political, and economic equality as a threat to their masculinity. Students might debate whether masculinity itself is socially and economically defined. In paragraphs 8 through 12, Faludi offers copious evidence to show that the "masculinity crisis" is a recurring and therefore exaggerated crisis that American men have survived many times.

3. Having a good income (or good prospects) is something many women tend to look for in a man—although this is changing somewhat as independent women seek younger men as partners. Aside from the obvious value of materialism, this economic definition of masculinity subscribes to the notion of the male as head of the household. Students might discuss what other notions of masculinity either complement or contradict this idea of man as good provider.

4. Faludi's entire essay illustrates how carefully one must argue to make a good case in support of a controversial claim. In this section, Faludi's assertion of an economic basis of the backlash is supported with extensive well-documented evidence. Students might check the Works Cited section of the article (pp. 391–393) to see how many sources she used. Note that she relies heavily on two surveys: the American Male Opinion Index and the Yankelovich Monitor survey. Students might want to find out more on how these were conducted. Because it appears so solid, students might discuss how Faludi's argument could be challenged. Would a first step be trying to find evidence to the contrary? Where would they begin?

5. Students may need help paraphrasing Faludi's argument about how various advertisers have exploited feminism to appeal to women consumers. They identify the product with feminism, even if the product has no possible benefits to the cause of women's equality. And they argue that shopping and buying—consuming—give women power. Students should debate the evidence: How common is this conception? What ads do they find that support or refute it? They might begin by discussing whether the advertisement on page 407 for Lawman Jeans is an example of what Faludi is talking about.

Cartoon by Kirk Anderson (Page 395)

The title of the cartoon implies that the gains made by the feminist movement in the 1960s and 1970s have been significantly eroded in the 1980s and 1990s. The definition of feminism expressed in the cartoon assumes that gender discrimination violates the principle of equal treatment under the law. The cartoon effectively persuades, in our opinion, because it warns its readers (especially women) that complacency or "lip service" endorsements of feminism will strengthen the forces of gender discrimination in our society. You might ask students to survey a number of their female friends, asking whether they consider themselves feminists. They might then discuss how common is the perception that feminists are "radicals" or "extremists."

Wolf, "The Beauty Myth" (Pages 396–405)

1.   Wolf's case that beauty standards are cultural rather than objective and biological appears in paragraphs 9–12. Her reasons are (1) different cultures have different ideas of what is beautiful, including what is sexually attractive and which gender is the more provocative; and (2) Darwin saw the idea of "sexual selection" in humans as an aberration from his theory of natural selection. Her evidence is largely from the field of anthropology. Should she have used more evidence from biology? Students might want to research this topic in more depth. Some recent cross-cultural studies of "beauty" in facial features have shown that symmetry and certain proportions are appreciated similarly across ethnic groups. Would evidence from art history have helped or hurt Wolf's case? What other evidence might support the idea that "beauty" is unrelated to sexual selection for reproduction?

2.   *The political argument:* In support of her view that the beauty myth was intended to keep women subordinate in power to men, Wolf shows that images of beauty were just one of many "fictions" that had the effect of keeping women inside the domestic sphere. Paragraph 16 lists other such fictions. Paragraph 20 presents Wolf's argument about the political reasons for the current resurfacing of the beauty myth. *The economic argument:* Paragraph 25 offers current economic reasons for keeping women in the position of being "worth less" than men. Students might compare this argument with Faludi's argument that economic conditions have led to the "backlash" against feminism.

3.   You might want to read or summarize material from the later chapters of Wolf's book. Her chapter on eating disorders is compelling, as is the chapter on plastic surgery. Certainly, material consumption is another behavior students might cite as desirable in our society today. What beauty characteristics today would symbolize this behavior? As this book went to press, for example, the fashion industry was promoting a waif-like image of beauty with undersized, childish fashions, little-girl hair styles, and prepubescent body images. What behavior in women does this image suggest is desirable?

4.   In this excerpt, Wolf seems to deny that makeup, exercise, and fashion could ever enhance women's lives, even though she later went on to say that they could. Apparently, she would argue for an idea of beauty that encourages women's individuality and self-confidence, rather than one that forces women to conform to a set ideal.

Two Ads for Women's Jeans (Pages 406–407)

You might want to read our discussion of visual persuasion on pages 29–30 of this manual, where we discuss the two advertisements.

Chapter 13

Answers to Questions: Sexual Harassment

Equal Employment Opportunity Commission, "Title VII Guidelines on Sexual Harassment" (Pages 412–414)

1. A sexual advance might well be unexpected, even shocking, but one's response could nonetheless be ambivalent: flattered but uninterested or intrigued but prevented by moral scruples from responding. If a subordinate doesn't indicate in so many words that the advance is unwelcome, the harasser may well conclude that just the timing or choice of place is wrong. We believe that a consistent pattern of avoidance or rejection ought to indicate that the attention is unwelcome.

2. "Verbal or physical conduct of a sexual nature" could include put-downs of women as a group or of individual women; groping, patting, or even hugging; sexual jokes; and displays of sexually explicit material. All of these can threaten or intimidate, whether the intention is conscious or not. But surely intent does and should matter, at least in some of these cases. Some men are less formal and more spontaneously affectionate than others, just as some women are more easily offended or threatened than others. In any case, when an individual indicates disapproval, the "verbal or physical conduct" should cease.

3. Clearly, criteria have to be relevant to the people involved, so the "reasonable woman" test—though analogous to other vague legal tests—really doesn't help much. What helps is actual court rulings in specific cases. These establish precedents at least for legal judgments about the nature or quality of behavior. Another good test may be whether or not a majority or at least a sizeable percentage of women working in a particular environment find it "intimidating, hostile, or offensive."

4. The guidelines recognize how relative things are in a culture such as ours which lacks universally applicable social norms for conduct between the sexes. Hence, one looks for patterns of abuse, tries to judge from context, and, as always, is wary of hearsay and the unsubstantiated. Circumstances can certainly make the same act more or less serious. A sexual caress is one thing after hours, between employees who are friendly and of the same rank; it is quite another from a boss one hardly knows. Direct witness would certainly indicate knowledge, but a pattern of behavior over time involving many people may also indicate that an employer "knows or should have known" that abuse was taking place. Responsibility of this kind is a given of supervisory positions.

5. Employers can protect themselves by "taking immediate and appropriate corrective action" against offenders, such as reprimands, loss of pay or status, even dismissal. The intent of the law is to discourage authorities from "looking the other way," from ignoring the problem, which is a major reason the problem exists. Furthermore, a pattern of sexual harassment over time is

difficult not to know about, so that the extent of liability seems defensible, fair, and just. Certainly an employee who becomes aware that her status was negatively affected by sexual harassment should have legal recourse.

University of Minnesota, "Policy Statement on Sexual Harassment" (Pages 415–417)

1. Paragraph 4 especially shows the professorial viewpoint, but not inappropriately and not to the exclusion of other people who attend or work at universities. The omission may indicate a lack of agreement about procedures and/or the lack of authority to institute such procedures. Obviously, procedures would include some oversight office where students and staff can lodge their complaints and some judicial body to hear them and recommend or enforce punishment.

2. The ethical problem is due to the unequal status of students and faculty. Young students may develop "crushes" on older faculty who can take advantage of their inexperience and insecurity. A sexual relationship is not quite consensual in the ordinary sense when the people cannot relate to each other roughly as equals. For this reason, even "consensual" sexual relations between faculty and undergraduates are, in our experience, generally viewed with disapproval. Graduate students, however, are another matter, especially when the faculty member and the student are close in age and unattached. Few people at universities seem to perceive problems in such cases.

3. Since many first-year students have no experience with faculty-student interaction at colleges, this question may require a special approach. Have students talk about how they related to favorite high school teachers, especially ones they had contact with out of class. Talk about close and "professionally appropriate" relationships you had with your college professors. Then imagine what would constitute "too close," and what sort of reasoning would justify such a judgment.

The New Republic, "Talking Dirty" (Pages 418–421)

1. Certainly, the first and last incidents would not qualify, and maybe not the third. The point here is that some very offensive behavior that no one could excuse falls under the "hostile environment" clause. It may be vague, but can we do without it?

2. One line of reasoning: No one should have to endure offensive language or behavior. In some cases, however, we can simply leave and not return, thereby avoiding what offends us. But we all have to make a living, and for most of us this means going to some public place which we can't avoid without losing our jobs. Therefore, offensive language and behavior ought to be prohibited, especially when it interferes with job performance.

3. We cannot see how the one is any harder to gauge than the other, unless perhaps job performance is more quantifiable in terms of days missed, declines in productivity, and so forth. But poor performance can have many causes. We see no way around "difficult, subjective" judgments in sexual harassment cases. And even if it could be eliminated, we think the "hostile environment" clause protects women from a common form of abuse.

Dziech and Weiner, "Sexual Harassment on Campus" (Pages 422–434)

1. Among the explanations offered are the following:
    a. Failure of victims to report abuse.
    b. Denial or conscious ignoring of the problem by authorities.
    c. Lack of careful study of the problem.
    d. Uncertainty about what "sexual harassment" is.

    We list these in what we consider the order of decreasing importance. The first is a major problem, since recent studies show continuing reluctance to report abuse.

2. We agree that sexual harassment can be trivialized by the way it is discussed, especially by men. But we also know professors who will not close their office door if alone with a student. Even if false accusations of sexual harassment are rare—and they seem to be—careers can be damaged seriously by accusation alone. There are many grey areas. When, for example, does enthusiastic admiration become sexual harassment?

3. We consider the distinction quite sound, the difference between hassle and harassment being a difference in power. It is certainly wrong to equate the exploitation of students by professors with student crushes and flirtatious behavior toward professors. Nor does sexual hassle excuse sexual harassment. However, professors *are* human, and we wonder if it is realistic to expect them not to respond to provocative behavior from students. What exactly is "irresponsible behavior" in such circumstances? College students are not children. And not all male professors are as confident and as powerful as they are depicted here.

Davidson, "Feminism and Sexual Harassment" (Pages 435–444)

1. Apparently a high percentage of women experience some form of sexual harassment. All of them are not feminists, yet surely their mistreatment is a serious issue for them. We know many more or less traditional women—and not a few men—who are very strongly opposed to sexual harassment. No, the issue cannot be dismissed as a feminist issue.

2. It seems foolish to argue that there are no inherent differences between the sexes when there obviously are differences in the nature and function of the sex organs, in hormones, in reproductive functions, in average size and strength, in

voice timbre, and so on. The difficulty is not in recognizing difference, but in distinguishing relative degrees of inherence and social construction, and detecting to what extent apparently inherent traits are exaggerated or codified through socialization.

3.   Historically, *feminine* has been defined as unassertive, nurturing, peace-making, sensitive, easily influenced, and passive. A kind of aggressive overcompensation might qualify as "female chauvinism," as well as the common assertion that females are actually superior to males—better able to handle pain, more emotionally self-sufficient, and so forth. But advocating an equality *of power* between the sexes need not entail female chauvinism, any more than sharing power need diminish masculine qualities.

4.   We perceive and appreciate the contradiction and agree that it won't do. But there is another way to sum up feminist philosophy: Feminists hold that men and women are different, that the qualities of both should be appreciated without prejudice, and that gender differences should have nothing to do with distinctions in power in either public or private life. Power is the issue, and men having a far greater measure of power simply because they are men is the problem. Surely this outlook can be found among feminists, so it is not necessarily the case that feminism is self-contradictory.

5.   As described, the class sounds indefensible from an academic point of view. The author's appeal to a conservative audience is obvious, but the relevance of the example is questionable. Odd classes are tolerated on college campuses sometimes, but oddities hardly establish norms, and men on college campuses are far more often harassers than harassed. The argument is specious.

Chapter 14

Answers to Questions: Abortion and Religion

Spero, "Therefore Choose Life: How the Great Faiths View Abortion" (Pages 448–461)

1. "Elective abortion" usually refers to a woman's choosing to end a normal pregnancy when both she and the fetus are in good health. Foes of abortion argue that women often "elect" abortions just because a pregnancy is inconvenient, a motivation they suggest lacks value when compared with the value of human life. But elective abortions need not be thoughtless or irresponsible. And "extreme conditions" are hard to define. How ill must the mother be? How impaired the fetus? Is a child conceived by incest or rape an extreme condition?

2. Basically Catholicism is the most restrictive and, according to Spero, does not permit "direct abortion" even to save the mother's life. Judaism, fundamentalist Protestantism, and Islam permit abortion when the mother's life is in danger. Some Jewish, Protestant, and Islamic authorities sanction abortion in cases of psychological distress or when conception occurs from rape or incest. Finally, some Protestant groups are strongly pro-choice, allowing abortion for social, economic, and family reasons. It is probably true that all the great faiths find abortion very problematical morally, but not necessarily "abhorrent." Some obviously regard state intervention in the reproductive choices of women more objectionable than the act of abortion itself. Spero does not emphasize this enough.

3. It is true that Spero recognizes diversity of opinion in all the faiths. One can cite from many places in the article to confirm this. However, he does not seem to emphasize enough how moral questions can be outweighed by other values, such as freedom of choice. Spero's approach is almost theocratic, attempting to wrest the various views into alignment, so far as possible, with his own. Many church authorities, even Catholic ones, find traditional prohibitions unrealistic in modern contexts and out of touch with current social and political realities.

Anderson, "Abortion and the Churches: 'Clarification' or Rollback?" (Pages 462–470)

1. We would say that abortion is unquestionably a means of birth control, control by elimination. But the phrase "abortion as birth control" implies that some—too many—women get abortions rather than practicing pre-conceptive birth control. We know of women who have done so, but the vast majority are not so irresponsible, and the distress that many women say follows an abortion suggests that rather than a "mere convenience," it is a most difficult and painful choice. It seems to us that even very responsible people get pregnant and that when they opt for abortion it is dehumanizing to dismiss such a decision as mere convenience.

2.   We take the charge of gender, race, and class bias quite seriously. Many of our churches draw much of their membership from a narrow range of people in our society. Some churches do not permit women to occupy positions of authority, in effect excluding any direct input from women in the debate over abortion. Given these facts, a degree of bias is inevitable. However, bias can also be detected, acknowledged, and compensated for; furthermore, since bias cannot be entirely eliminated, it is not per se a reason to reject viewpoints out of hand. All opposition to abortion certainly cannot be written off as sexism, racism, or classism.

3.   Laws banning abortion completely would impose the most restrictive Catholic view; those allowing exceptions would not impose a single religious view because a wide spectrum of theological opinion allows for exceptions. One need not be religious in any conventional sense to oppose abortion under most circumstances—some humanists, for example, see life as the highest value, but deny the existence of God and the claims of church authority. In conceptual terms, then, laws restricting abortion need not be a violation of church and state. In reality, however, it is overwhelmingly the religious right that agitates against abortion; should that view prevail, one could argue, a whole ideology— religious, political, and social—would be imposed on all women. We view this as unacceptable in any democracy and unconstitutional in ours.

Kissling, "Ending the Abortion War: A Modest Proposal" (Pages 471–478)

1.   While we recognize that all of her proposals can be disputed, we find them well-informed, intelligent, and persuasive. Certainly, we agree that the main goals are to develop more reliable methods of birth control and facilitate more informed decision-making about pregnancies—and that the government should take a positive role. We also agree that pro-choice advocates cannot oppose all regulation of abortion, post-viability abortions being a good case in point. Her proposals do seem to us to take what she calls the "tragedy" of abortion seriously, and so to equal her high moral sense of the problem.

2.   The main differences between Kissling's argument and Rosenblatt's have to do with audience and purpose. Kissling is writing to pro-choice advocates, to convince them to see the *Roe v. Wade* decision as "a framework for good policy on abortion, not as a fortress against policy" (paragraph 17). Kissling is primarily interested in proposing policies that would acknowledge the complexity of abortion. Rosenblatt is writing to interested people on all sides of the issue, to convince them that the contradictory interests, values, and beliefs behind opposing sides of the debate need to be respected and tolerated in a policy that permits but discourages abortion. Kissling looks more at specific current policy debates, such as those over public funding, while Rosenblatt situates the debate more intellectually, in the history of ideas. Rosenblatt seems to be arguing primarily for a change in attitude, and secondarily for new policies. The main similarity between the two is that both see the solution as a

process of learning to live with tension and conflict. Kissling, in paragraph 12, explains this as a tension between women's rights to decide and society's concern over both fetal life and women's sound decision-making. In paragraph 9 of his essay, Rosenblatt argues that Americans need to learn to live with ambivalence. Rosenblatt's essay is more likely to break down the barriers between sides on the issue, mainly because it is less specific. Both Kissling and Rosenblatt suggest ways to reduce the need for abortion, as both see this as the ultimate solution to the problem.

3. In the long run, we think the chances are quite good. Assuming that abortions are not made illegal again, Kissling's cool-headed, rational approach ought to prevail. Some regulation of abortion is inevitable, without prohibiting abortions in the early months of pregnancy. The central concern should be to create conditions within which informed, moral decisions can be made. We find in her balancing of rights and ethical concerns a hope for the future.

Chapter 15

Answers to Questions: Race Relations: Where Are We Now?

Photograph by Bruce Roberts (Page 481)

The photograph offers a historical record of a time before the Civil Rights Movement when segregation was both the law in some parts of the country and morally defensible in the view of many whites. Constructed by a white majority, the bathroom facilities sent a message to both whites and blacks in the pre–civil rights South: Whites are fully human, with gender differences that matter and a need for privacy worth respecting, while blacks are less than human, being neither "men" nor "women," but "colored."

Kapuscinski, "Second Thoughts about America's Racial Paradise" (Pages 482–486)

1. "Openness" might be defined as being secure enough in one's own viewpoints to be willing to listen seriously to others and to be willing to change one's views as a result of dialogue with others. It need not mean a lack of convictions or an "anything goes" attitude. "Pluralism" means a *principled* entertaining of a number of perspectives—it can be contrasted with eclecticism, or the "grocery cart" approach, which borrows whatever it wants without concern for how various points of view fit together. "The polycentric mind" implies an intellect that has overcome ethnocentricism and can consequently feel at home among many kinds of people. Except for those raised in Los Angeles, New York, or like places, the mix of languages, colors, and cultures can exhaust, overwhelm, or even terrify. People can feel a vague sense of threat, often associated with the unfamiliar.

2. Ethnocentricity is the restriction of one's viewpoint to the norms and values of a single group—say, white, middle-class people of northern European origin. It can be the "mentality of destruction" in that such notions of identity have played a major role in repression of minority groups (including genocide), in colonialism, and in wars. Given the division of neighborhoods in Los Angeles and elsewhere in the United States by racial and class groups, we may doubt that the tribal mentality has been overcome. Perhaps the real challenge is maintaining one's identity without being ethnocentric, while insisting on fair treatment for all. In this way ethnocentricity need not be the mentality of destruction.

3. Compared with "the destructive, paralyzed Third World," our racial problems are certainly less acute than was the case even thirty years ago. Kapuscinski's comparative judgment cannot be dismissed. Nor does our contribution to Third World problems invalidate the general comparison. We tend to gauge conditions in the United States by our own ideals of "liberty and justice for all" and find actual conditions wanting—as indeed we should. But compared to the terrible carnage in the Middle East and in what was Yugoslavia, the United States—

4. We could view all three as "centrisms," but fixated on different kinds of identity. The last is the hardest to specify, but it amounts to what Kenneth Burke calls the most dangerous motivation of all, religiosity gone bad. It is typified by rigid doctrine and absolutely no tolerance for anyone who does not adhere to that doctrine, and poses the threat of "holy war" wherever it exists, because the "infidel" must be either converted or destroyed. There is no flashpoint anywhere in the world not traceable to these centrisms, and no significant source of social unrest and strife in the United States wholly free of them. One need only examine the news on any given day to confirm the explosiveness of the three powder kegs Kapuscinski singles out for special attention.

Killian, "Race Relations and the Nineties: Where Are the Dreams of the Sixties?" (Pages 487–501)

1. The conditions Killian describes are real and fully justify his glum outlook. At the same time, assessments like Killian's were particularly common in the Reagan and Bush years, which saw the general plight of blacks grow worse rather than better. Social liberals or progressives tend to be more hopeful and less critical when Democrats control the White House.

2. Killian sees the Civil Rights Movement as largely successful in eliminating segregation and securing voting rights. But the material condition of black people is still unequal. Killian credits the separatist Black Power Movement with creating the "novel concept" of "ethnic group rights" (paragraph 9), but otherwise failing to achieve its goal of black rule. The conflict between civil rights and black power continues in the ideological conflict between individual rights and policies on behalf of historically oppressed groups, such as affirmative action. It also continues in the conflict between blacks who desire to assimilate with white society and those who insist on a separate identity, marked by black pride in black culture.

3. The "equality of anonymity" refers to nominal equality but practical segregation, as well as the loss of identity that results from the loss of an energizing cause as an organized force for change. To some extent awareness of black identity is higher on college campuses today, both among blacks and among faculty and administrators who are not black. But how we evaluate this activism (if we can call it that) depends on whether we want to diminish racial differences or preserve them.

4. We think Edna Bonacich's view is essentially accurate. Our society not only tolerates but even demands vast disparities in wealth. Blacks do suffer disproportionately, but as she says, even if they were represented proportionately in all economic classes, the suffering of the underclass would remain. We can detect, then, that economic repression goes hand in hand with racial repression; probably the problem is more fundamentally grounded in class than race. If so, we face the perhaps insurmountable problem that our

individualist-capitalist ideology will scarcely tolerate socialistic sharing of the wealth.

Davis, "Challenge for the Year 2000" (Pages 502–508)

1. Compare the caves metaphor with paragraphs 20–22 and 41–43 in Killian and with the paragraph on Bonacich (36). Our ghettos are the caves, and their function of exclusion, of keeping the underside of our society out of sight and out of mind, safely away from the relatively privileged, seems indisputable.

2. King's uneasiness with the need for power is shown in his yoking of power to the purposes of "love and justice." The anti-idealistic notion of a naked power struggle—the issue being simply, who runs things?—was faced more directly by the black power movement, if not necessarily with greater rhetorical appeal to whites. The idea that power is or can be joined with love and justice seems to cynical minds almost naive—power is getting the lion's share for one's self and one's allies—but the defiant honesty of black power tends to increase resistance rather than work toward empowerment. So we can argue about realism here. King's approach may be more rhetorically realistic.

3. The "psychological violence" comes from constant reminders of inferior status in everything across the board—food, shelter, medical services, city services—which cumulatively wear down the spirits of the poor. What we see as we travel through the poor parts of our cities is a pervasive hopelessness, a despair that must contribute to the appeal of drugs and drug money. Periodically the frustration breaks out in violence, mostly blacks against blacks, but sometimes also in police violence, itself related to frustration. This genocidal siege has much to do with the subtler "psychological violence" of ghetto conditions.

4. The global view is, interestingly enough, the view that Malcolm X came to hold. There can be no question that the often desperate conditions of black Africans share common sources with the conditions of the black underclass in the United States. However, this enlightened understanding is a hard sell: Privileged Americans dissociate the United States from the Third World, and many blacks simply do not feel a kinship with Africa. The cultural connections have weakened over four centuries, and blacks here are likely to ask, quite realistically, what will linking all of it together do for me?

Raspberry, "The Myth That Is Crippling Black America" (Pages 509–511)

1. Raspberry shares with black power advocates the insistence that blacks must not depend on the benevolence of others but on themselves. But Raspberry works within the ideology of individualism, not of collective identity—the militant organization of a race—which inspired black power. The difference in essence is this: Raspberry says to the poor black, "It's up to you," whereas black power says, "It's up to us."

2. The comparison isn't fair because the background of the Asian immigrant does not include slavery, and while prejudice against Asians certainly exists, it has usually not been as extreme and systematic as it has been against blacks. Furthermore, to say that blacks have been born in the candy store is hardly accurate; for the most part they have been on the outside in a more painful way than people outside the United States who want to come here. The analogy is certainly common and presumably persuasive among whites, but the comparison tends only to generate racial tensions between blacks and Asians rather than to inspire blacks to self-improvement.

3. As noted before, King's socialistic program for improving the conditions of poor blacks probably has very little chance of capturing the imaginations of most Americans. Raspberry's solution is actually more likely to bear fruit, for it conforms to the prevailing system: Economic power translates very readily into power generally in our society. The problem, however, is that the entrepreneurial route is open only to the brightest and most energetic in any ethnic or racial group, so that his solution is at best a very partial one.

4. We think there's some truth in the accusation. Genuine sympathy and concern for the millions of poor people in the United States is rare enough among the successful, regardless of race. But we also think the cold reality is that self-help and cooperation within black communities are the best long-range hope in a society that fosters gross economic inequality.

Steele, "The Recoloring of Campus Life" (Pages 512–524)

1. Basically "racial equality" means that blacks are not discriminated against because they are black—at least not systematically. Steele supports this contention by pointing out that blacks are not now excluded from classes, housing, or extracurricular activities. Indeed, black students are often heavily recruited by predominantly white colleges, offered scholarships, provided with tutors, and provided other benefits. But racial prejudice among both students and faculty still exists, and the education blacks receive before college is often markedly inferior to what whites receive.

2. Steele depicts the politics of difference as a divisive force that thrives on mystification of difference and that tends to rekindle long-established racial prejudices. We believe Steele thinks much as King did: People should be judged by the content of their characters rather than by the color of their skin. Ideally, race should no more be remarked on than, say, whether one is right or left handed. And so he argues against race as a source of power for anyone and against "difference" departments. It seems to us that there has always been a politics of difference, and always will be, both on and off college campuses. We cannot find fault with women and minorities claiming some of the power traditionally denied them.

3. Steele sees in black power an absolute demand for entitlement, a view he condemns, considering it both unreasonable and destructive to the end he wants:

total integration, genuine community. Killian also sees group entitlement as a goal of black power but salutes this as a concept that has helped blacks gain a chance at success. They differ ideologically, Steele seeing society as a struggle of individuals, Killian as a struggle of classes and races. Steele's view appeals idealistically, drawing on deep-seated American values; Killian appeals realistically, through emphasis on the concrete economic and social realities of racial and class conflict. Since adopting Killian's view would mean rejecting capitalism and individualism, most Americans will find Steele's the more attractive.

4.   Both Steele and Raspberry apparently have completely integrated—materially and spiritually—with white society; so much so, that many blacks would probably say they aren't black anymore. They have played the system and played it successfully—hence, understandably, they endorse it: individualism, capitalism, and all.

5.   We think Steele has hit the mark here with the notion of "a suspicion of incomplete humanity" and an acknowledgment that such attitudes have collective sources and historical realities behind them. Furthermore, it seems to us that the fear of inferiority applies, *mutatis mutandis,* to women, homosexuals, and other minority races, as does the defensiveness of white males toward the spoken or unspoken accusation of unfair advantage. But if the problem is collective, mustn't the solution be so too? Does Steele's acute analysis of the new racism fit his let-difference-disappear prescription?

Chapter 16

Answers to Questions: Gay and Lesbian Rights

Nickel, "Everybody's Threatened by Homophobia" (Pages 527–530)

1. We suspect that men may be more aware of the culture's homophobia than women. If your students' experiences have convinced them that Nickel is right, they should discuss how and when this prejudice was conveyed to them. You might also talk about the extent to which the media and other influences might be projecting a more positive image of homosexuality and whether this may influence children to be less afraid of homosexuality.

2. While some media figures like Madonna and Janet Jackson speak and sing openly about their sexuality, in our society women are expected to be sexy, but not sexual. As Nickel states, they may concern themselves with pleasing men, but it is unfeminine to talk about what pleases them. There are women who don't even know about orgasms because this is such a taboo subject that they can't talk about it among themselves.

3. Nickel speaks of straight friends who have confided in him, and this fact shows that he is a concerned listener. Further, his sympathy for his grade school classmate (paragraph 5) is apparent in the detail with which he recalls the humiliating incident he describes.

4. Some of the most obvious persuasive devices are Nickel's allusion to Allen Ginsburg's poem and to the work of Holocaust survivor Elie Weisel, both of whom would likely be familiar to his readers. Also, Nickel uses specific details in recounting the incidents that serve as evidence throughout the argument. Finally, Nickel's tone is informal; he seems to be speaking directly to his audience, as a friend.

Hamill, "Confessions of a Heterosexual" (Pages 531–536)

1. We believe that the economic connection still exists. In general, working-class people tend to be fairly parochial. Education and exposure to a wide range of opinions, such as occurs in college, tend to increase tolerance and destroy stereotypes, as was true in Hamill's case (paragraph 15).

2. In a society where it is socially acceptable to beat up a whole category of people, it is clearly to those people's advantage to remain invisible if possible. Even today, for the gay men and lesbian women who have come out of the closet, beatings are still common.

3. In paragraphs 15, 16, and 17, Hamill describes how he overcame his homophobia. Some of your students might have had similar experiences; meeting and getting to know gay people, or discovering that someone you know and like is homosexual, is a powerful means of overcoming homophobia, but it can happen only if homosexuals come out of the closet.

4. In paragraphs 19–23, Hamill explains that gay activists' "rantings" about AIDS have changed his perspective on "everything about homosexuals." However, students might note that the incident with which he opens his essay is a gay march in protest of gay-bashing, including the planting of a bomb. And he also notes in paragraph 9 that he is tired of people who identify themselves "exclusively by what they do with their cocks." (Is their sexual activity what makes them different?) In that same paragraph, he says that he and other liberals still look upon gays with "a mixture of uneasiness and contempt." In other words, it is not just AIDS.

    Hamill uses such terms as "paranoid oratory," "self-pitying aura of victimhood" (paragraph 20), "cheap pity," and "romantic bullshit" (paragraph 26) to describe the language used by gay activists. Does he give any examples of this language besides what he offers in paragraphs 2 and 3? We would find his evidence more convincing if he named some gay activist leaders and quoted from their speeches and writings.

5. Hamill is asking the homosexual community to tone down its rhetoric, especially its verbal attacks on the straight community (paragraph 26). He calls for unity rather than division, but he makes no specific suggestions about what gay and straight people ought to do to reduce homophobia.

Cartoon by Tom Meyer (Page 537)

The Navy officer in Meyer's cartoon is being airlifted off his podium by the fighter plane, representing the Tailhook scandal. The fact that heterosexual debauchery had been a feature of the Tailhook conventions over the years and that only one officer was held responsible for the 1991 incidents indicates that sexual harassment was, for many aviators, an acceptable activity. Students might discuss whether being offensive to women is part of the stereotype of the aggressive male.

Gomes, "Homophobic? Reread Your Bible" (Pages 538–541)

1. Gomes simply places the commonly quoted Bible passages into the literal context that surrounds them. He does not dispute that the passages from Leviticus and the gospels of St. Paul prohibit homosexual acts, but he explains that these prohibitions are part of a larger set of rules that includes prohibitions which seem irrelevant or hard to defend in contemporary American society. This strategy allows him to move into the main part of his argument, which is about selective interpretation of the Bible for ideological reasons.

2. In paragraph 12, Gomes states that the "right use of the Bible . . . means that we confront our prejudices rather than merely confirm them." On pages 42 through 44, we explain that before we can take a stand or defend a position that we already hold, we must inquire into the truth of that position, acknowledging our own biases. A "right" interpretation of Scripture, to Gomes, is an interpretation motivated by the desire to understand and appreciate the will of God, not the desire to justify one's political position. As such, it would be an interpretation that advocates inclusiveness, not intolerance.

3. In paragraphs 17 through 20, Gomes gives a series of examples, pieces of evidence for his case that right interpretation is liberating, wrong interpretation destructive. The contrasting interpretations on each topic are emphasized by Gomes's stylistic device of balanced sentences, each beginning with the repeated words "the same Bible."

4. Fear works as a persuader, whether it is fear of having bad breath, fear of getting lung cancer, or fear of dying in an alcohol-related car crash. The issue is not whether it should be used, but rather whether making people afraid is justified. Is the threat real? Whose good will be served by making the appeal? In other words, you should inquire about facts, motives, and implications before making appeals to fear.

5. One of the most obvious is the issue of abortion. In Rabbi Aryeh Spero's essay, "Therefore Choose Life: How the Great Faiths View Abortion" (pages 448–461), students can find some of the passages often cited from the Bible and from the Koran by people opposed to abortion rights. Another is the place of women in the family; people in favor of "traditional values" cite such verses as Genesis 2:21–23, which describe God's creation of Eve from the rib of Adam, and Genesis 3:16, in which God tells Eve, "thy desire shall be to thy husband, and he shall rule over thee." Divorce was permitted among the Old Testament Jews, but in the Sermon on the Mount, Jesus speaks against it (Matthew 5:31–32). Also, the place of women in the church is debated based on Scripture. While many New Testament passages show that women were active in the early church, other verses can be found that say women should be silent in the church. Other issues are conscientious objection to military service, capital punishment, and the relationship of humans to the environment, especially our relationship to other animals. Indeed, there is almost no issue for which one cannot find a pertinent Bible passage, even the question of hair length (1 Corinthians 11:14–15). Students might want to apply Gomes's criteria for "right" use of Scripture to some of these arguments.

Alter, "Degrees of Discomfort" (Pages 542–544)

1. Alter believes that people ought to be able to disapprove of homosexual acts on moral grounds but still allow these acts to be legal and ensure that homosexual people not be discriminated against in any way. He supports this by separating the homosexual act (which it is acceptable to disapprove of) from

the homosexual person (whom it is not acceptable to disapprove of). Thus, he shows that homophobia is not the same as racism, which is always anti-person, rather than anti-act.

2. Alter's argument is that homosexuals not having sex are like cigarette smokers not smoking. In other words, they are all just people who may engage in sexual or smoking behaviors at other times. This seems like a reasonable analogy to us, since it holds true for heterosexuals as well.

3. While homosexuals must keep their sexuality hidden, heterosexuals flaunt theirs openly. Heterosexuality is so obvious a part of our culture that it is not consciously noticed. Advertising shows couples kissing and embracing, always heterosexual. American sporting events and parades are embellished with women in obviously sexual costumes, meant to attract the attention of male spectators. Students might discuss how they feel about public displays of affection in general. Our point here is to get students to think about a double standard that defines what straight people do as "normal" but calls "obnoxious" or "perverted" the exact same behavior when it is done by homosexuals.

4. We would question the distinction between person and behavior that allows Alter to make this claim. If a genetic basis for homosexuality exists, as seems more and more likely, to disapprove of the act seems equivalent to racism, for one is making a judgment about something that is innate, just like race. After all, denying people the right to their own sexuality deprives them of part of their humanity.

5. This is a difficult question to answer without more research; however, Isay's theory receives some support from the fact that women tend to be more tolerant of homosexuality than do men. Women are less likely to fear discovering in themselves some traits that our culture defines as "masculine" than men are to fear discovering traits that our culture calls "feminine."

Levin, "A Case against Civil Rights for Homosexuals" (Pages 545–546)

1. According to Levin, people should have the right not to "associate" with homosexuals if homosexuality is an affront to their moral or religious principles. It seems that this argument hinges on the definition of the word "associate," since no "anti-discrimination" laws would require private contact, such as socializing, but rather have to do with public contact, such as at work or school. Students might want to debate the differences. You might note that in paragraph 2, Levin extends this concept of freedom of conscience to include the anti-Semite's right not to employ a Jew.

2. He is suggesting that homosexuals can avoid discrimination by hiding their sexual preferences, just as Jews can hide their religion if they are worried about anti-Semitism. (A philosopher and a Jew himself, Levin is being more

theoretical here than practical. He wants to be totally consistent in his defense of the "sovereignty of individual conscience" so that abortion-rights supporters can see the inconsistency of their position.)

3. Students might debate the degree to which one's sexuality is an integral part of one's personality—even when one is not in a sexual situation. For example, bringing a lover or companion to a party indicates one's sexual orientation. Also, students should consider the awkward social situations that might confront a gay or lesbian person whose friends and colleagues assumed that he or she was straight. And students might consider the "common good" that is served by hiding or disclosing difference of any kind.

Mohr, "The Civic Rights of Invisible Minorities" (Pages 547–552)

1. Mohr's argument seems aimed more at convincing than persuading; readers of the book that it is excerpted from would already be interested in issues of justice for gay and lesbian people. Therefore, to accomplish his aim, he does not need to build a great deal of sympathy for the victims in his hypothetical case. In fact, what he needs to do is show a case that is representative of gay life.

2. Mohr points to the necessarily "public" nature of our judicial system, the effects of which would be felt by both the rape victim and the victim of gay-bashing. Like homosexuals who decline to press charges against their attackers, women are denied justice in rape cases when they are too humiliated by the experience to relive it in a courtroom or are afraid that a defense attorney will confront them with questions about their sex lives. Mohr would probably say that the main difference is that such public testimony in the case of the rape victim would not jeopardize her civil rights.

3. Any kind of civil case in which the person's sexual orientation could become an issue in the trial would serve as another example. Thus, a gay or lesbian parent who had children in a heterosexual marriage may decline to fight for child custody after a divorce. Or the gay or lesbian survivor named in his or her companion's will may not fight a family member's attempt to break the will.

4. Those who argue that homosexuals should not teach in grades K through 12 commonly support their case with two reasons: that homosexuals will influence youngsters to become homosexual by serving as improper role models and that they will seduce or molest their students. Students might begin by inquiring into the assumptions behind these reasons. One assumption for the first reason is that students would know that the teacher was homosexual, which is often not the case; another assumption is that homosexuality is a choice, that students would choose to become gay or lesbian because they admired a teacher who was. The second reason assumes that gay or lesbian teachers are more likely than straight teachers to exploit the student-teacher relationship for sexual purposes.

5. Moral debate may have preceded the passing of much legislation in our country, but the legal system protects everyone equally, in accordance with those laws. Thus, for example, abortion is a legal right. Those who hold that abortion is immoral cannot legally obstruct others from getting abortions or deny them any other of their civil rights. Gay people are often denied protection from the courts, however, in the 23 states with anti-sodomy laws. Anti-sodomy laws, which used to be common, but which have increasingly been repealed, are a perfect example of laws that were passed as a result of moral debate.

Rauch, "Beyond Oppression" (Pages 553–558)

1. No, we would not agree because the examples are clearly factual, and therefore objective by our definition of the word. Rauch has taken upon himself the authority to define oppression according to five criteria that he himself establishes. Even if we accept Rauch's criteria, it seems that many of the examples fit the first criterion, if not also some of the others. But we must recognize the power of Rauch's setting up the criteria, because he can pick and choose what constitutes oppression. If one cannot display a photograph of one's partner, is one not being denied the civil right of "pursuit of happiness"? Could this not be just as valid a criterion for claiming oppression?

2. See the answer to question 1 for a possible additional criterion. Ask your students to think of others. With respect to Rauch's second criterion, we would ask if a group's merely having the legal right to engage in political activity can constitute full political franchise if some members of the group fear that exercising that right will cause them to become victims of discrimination. Also, while access to education is not restricted by law, the learning environment in many institutions is hostile to those who are openly gay or lesbian. Rauch is admirably trying to draw the line between legitimate victims of oppression and pseudo-victims, but ultimately this distinction is subjective rather than objective.

3. He is asking individual homosexuals to make a difference by being open about their sexual orientation. He is asking for an attitude of pride that translates into action on a personal level. However, some of the actions he advocates, such as a "kiss-in," resemble the kinds of political activities endorsed by gay rights activists who are protesting what they see as oppression. We believe that individual action such as Rauch advocates may have the effect of influencing other individuals to overcome their homophobia; however, institutional discrimination against homosexuals is unlikely to be changed except by political action, as the Civil Rights Movement demonstrated.

Chapter 17

Answers to Questions: Political Correctness and Multiculturalism

Schlesinger, "The Cult of Ethnicity, Good and Bad" (Pages 563–565)

1. His audience is unquestionably the audience that reads *Time*—white, middle-class, traditional—and Schlesinger appeals to them by invoking pride in the specialness of America and in our general success, economically and politically. He also appeals to a deep fear that surfaces periodically when we have race riots in our cities: that our apparent unity as Americans could easily dissolve into ethnic divisiveness and conflict. Many will find his intelligent message of hope and optimism very persuasive.

2. "Cult," of course, is associated with religious fringe groups, often violent or threatening violence, and very deviant as judged by traditional norms. Obviously Schlesinger's choice of the word is designed to stimulate a negative reaction to the emphasis on ethnicity we see all around us. Ethnic "cult" thinking of the sort Schlesinger alludes to certainly exists, but we think it is not the great force some fear it to be. Most of the interest in ethnic "roots" seems to us harmless and superficial, perhaps a compensation for the perplexity of an America that now sees itself more problematically than it did prior to the Vietnam era.

3. This question is designed to get students to think more critically about the ideology of individualism. We suggest taking up some actual choices that students have made—the college they chose to attend, the car they drive, the activities they enjoy, where they live. How many of these choices are the result of non-individual influences, such as gender, class, race, or ethnic identity? What exactly is individual in our motives? How can I tell myself from the kinds of people I associate with? We think an individual is a unique combination of otherness, of the non-individual, so that an emphasis on ethnicity is not necessarily incompatible with individuality.

4. Romanticism, a rebellion against the Enlightenment, tends to emphasize natural sources of identity and value and to insist on the significance of the nonrational and irrational in human life. Romanticism has certainly fostered some dark moments in human history—the Nazis, for instance, in extolling "the folk" clearly were drawing on Romantic notions. So the category "romantic ideologues" is far from an empty generalization. We are not sure who fits the category of "unscrupulous con men." But we doubt that anyone can speak adequately for an entire race or ethnicity.

Cartoons by Garry Trudeau (Page 566)

Students should see the similarity between the Doonesbury cartoons and the points that Schlesinger makes in paragraphs 9 and 10 of his essay. Trudeau is mocking the tendency of Americans increasingly to see themselves as members of ethnic groups rather than as individuals and to demand their rights on the basis of their group membership.

"Whose Culture Is It, Anyway?"

Gates, "It's Not Just Anglo-Saxon" (Pages 567–568)
Kagan, "Western Values Are Central" (Pages 569–591)

1. Historically "our culture" has certainly not referred to the whole of the West, but mainly to the culture of northern Europe, especially Britain. It has tended to reject or underrate southern Europe, except for Italy and Greece, and to exclude Native Americans, blacks, and other minority groups. It seems to us that a global perspective is both necessary and desirable, so that Gates's point about "our culture" being only one of many in a world community of cultures is well-taken. Contrary to Gates's claim, however, both views are "politicized" in that any understanding of culture is always political.

2. Tolerance and respect for diversity is always a more or less relative notion. Historically, for example, Islamic culture has been more tolerant of religious differences than Christian culture has. One could hardly call our treatment of Native Americans "respect for diversity." On the other hand, no culture is more diverse than that of the United States, and we have certainly led the contemporary world in the direction of respect for human rights. It is also true that our advocacy of free speech—hardly a universal value—has made our culture a culture of self-criticism. Paradoxically, however, our educational system below the college level seems not to nurture critical attitudes of any kind, but rather a kind of contentless tolerance of everything and everybody.

3. Kagan might agree with Gates that culture is a conversation, and not let go of the centrality of Western values. After all, Western culture is itself a conversation among many identities or "voices." Gates would certainly have to grant that the West, backed by unprecedented economic and political influence for both good and ill, is "the most powerful paradigm" in the world. A genuine dialogue, then, could develop around the nature of Western culture and the kind of conversations it has or ought to have with non-Western cultures.

Ravitch, "Multiculturalism Yes, Particularism No" (Pages 572–576)

1. Probably Gates would say that the appeal to common humanity is deceptive in that "we" do not remake culture; rather the powerful, those in control, do, maintaining the overwhelmingly "regional culture" Gates mentions. Gates would say Ravitch is inattentive to power relations.

2. Separatism in such departments is probably to some extent unavoidable, though it certainly should not encourage exclusion of nonmembers from courses of study. It seems to us that courses in women's studies, for example, ought to emphasize the achievements of women and so foster self-esteem in female students that may have been raised to see themselves as inferior to men. But self-esteem is not inconsistent with self-criticism; rather, the only secure self-esteem is one that can endure its own self-doubts. We see no reason why pride and criticism cannot be combined.

3. A particularist in Ravitch's terminology is a racist or "ethnist" and therefore likely to be judged negatively by contemporary standards of broad, albeit not very thoughtful, tolerance. "Particularists" would probably see themselves as standing up for the powerless, the excluded or marginalized, the historically oppressed—people whose particular claims for recognition and acceptance still need to be made.

Van de Wetering, "Political Correctness: The Insult and the Injury" (Pages 577–584)

1. *Section One: Paragraphs 1–8*

    Deals with the definitions, backgrounds, and origins of political correctness; creates the context.

    Key moves include claiming that political correctness has been "misrepresented and misunderstood"; that "nomenclature is not devoid of significant history and education"; and that political correctness has not resulted in restrictions on freedom of speech.

    Section Two: Paragraphs 9–21

    Presents the case for political correctness and multiculturalism, defending them from their detractors.

    Key moves include claiming that political correctness addresses genuine problems; that free speech has civil and legal limits; that the fears of opponents are grounded in trivial misunderstandings of what America represents; and that multiculturalism is concerned with truth, "who we are."

    Section Three: Paragraphs 22–27

    Offers the conclusion, stating the desired changes in action and attitude and relating the argument to practical business concerns.

    Key moves include the association of political correctness and multiculturalism with inevitable and desirable change and the depiction of opponents as reactionaries; showing the crucial importance of "managing diversity"; and relating the issue to local conditions in Rochester.

The speaker uses all the resources of appeal in a reasonably skillful effort to *restructure* the preconceptions of his audience. Studied in this way, the speech provides a useful example of persuasive discourse.

2. Schlesinger would say that we have created a common American culture and therefore have not "failed at homogeneity"; Gates would agree, but would argue that this homogeneity is brought about by the suppression of difference; Kagan would presumably agree that a certain homogeneity in Western values exists but that it has to be shored up, preserved by educational practices; Ravitch would see the plurality in this alleged homogeneity and regard it as dynamic, rather than as a static given. Ravitch is nearest to Van de Wetering's view, though she would insist that we have not entirely failed in creating a common American culture.

3. There is much misunderstanding about "free speech." As long as we do not advocate sedition, we may criticize the government of the United States without fear of reprisal. But "free speech" has never meant and cannot mean that we are or should be excused from the general social consequences of what we say—and this includes strong disapproval of uncivil language, even exclusion from some groups or institutions based on what we say. This is routine, normal, and even "right" in the sense that acceptable speech has to be gauged not as an absolute, but in context.

D'Souza, "The Visigoths in Tweed" (Pages 585–593)

1. The general tone of the *Mother Jones* letter seems to us a bit overheated, but surely, after living through the 1980s, it is not bizarre at all to call attention to the impact of "greed, brutality, and indifference" on the poor in America, on the Third World, on the environment, and on the quality of our civil life generally. Perhaps the readers of *Forbes* will agree with D'Souza without argument, but we don't.

2. Racism, unfortunately, is not restricted to white people, though some of it exists in response to white racism and no doubt most of the damage is done by white racists who can back up their prejudice with power. As for the claim that all males are sexist, some are, in fact, feminists and actively, publicly so. While most men probably have at least some gender prejudice, Thompson's statement is too absolute to merit assent. At the same time, residual racism and sexism are too obviously present in most of us to be dismissed out of hand. Again, D'Souza is counting on his generally conservative readership to react as he wants them to, without argument.

3. Obviously we would need to know what percentage of students at Berkeley not admitted preferentially failed to graduate within five years. The figure is actually fairly high, we would guess, if Berkeley's graduation ratio is as low as that of many large, public institutions. Of course, one could also argue that, considering how inferior the education of many of our minorities is prior to

college, 30 percent is not so bad. The problem of keeping such students in school is a serious one, and most universities take it seriously.

4. Universities and university policy vary so much that we hesitate to generalize, but in our experience racial segregation is generally discouraged by campus authorities, which, of course, doesn't mean that de facto segregation doesn't exist regardless. We can only encourage racial integration; we cannot require it.

Ehrenreich, "What Campus Radicals?" (Pages 594–600)

1. Actually, our impression matches Ehrenreich's. Probably the lack of student concern means that no real problem exists at all. Right-wing critics of campus life do seem to find leftist conspiracies, even on campuses overwhelmingly dominated by moderate and conservative students and faculty. They seem to interpret a few prominent dissenting voices as representative of the whole.

2. Some faculty we know on both the left and right seem quite unable to listen to points of view incongruent with their own, and we imagine they do no better with students in their classes. Students sense such limitations and play the game, saying what their professors want to hear. Truly free and open discussion, rather than a professorial monologue, is only too rare in colleges, despite the fact that it is touted as a high value. We believe that nothing more extraordinary than overinflated egos is responsible for lack of open discussion.

3. We do agree that the quality of civil discourse has fallen, and that American politics is bland and boring. We are not sure how to account for it. Maybe part of the reason is the sound-bite mentality. Maybe part of it is the lack of central organizing issues of dissent, such as existed thirty years ago. Maybe part of it is the much-discussed "cultivate my own garden" outlook, hardly confined to college students. In any case, "rigid political conformity" usually masks a fear of thinking and a sense that collective norms are impaired and untrustworthy.

Cortés, "Pluribus and Unum: The Quest for Community amid Diversity" (Pages 601–608)

1. Whereas Ravitch dichotomizes, dissociating her notion of the multicultural from what she calls particularism, Cortés sees a necessary and permanent tension between his opposites, pluribus and unum. Consequently, he finds what he calls "group isolationism" understandable and tolerable so long as it is temporary. Otherwise, his multiculturalism is much like Ravitch's; perhaps he communicates a greater sense of profound struggle than she does.

2. We like the notion of "little loyalties"; we all have them, and, as Cortés contends, they help to maintain a sense of identity and belonging in a society altogether too rootless for human happiness. We would say such loyalties become extreme when there is no sense of larger community, or when the "little loyalties" cause outright rejection of the community as a whole, as in

some religious cults. We agree with the author that such extremism is avoidable, but we doubt that it is always avoided. Cortés probably doesn't deal realistically enough with the "us vs. them" mentality of some particularist groups.

3.   It is always difficult clearly to distinguish cases of "AC," especially since individuals differ so much in how flexible their ear is to different accents. In most cases we know of, "AC" combines with other problems—difficulty in the material itself and a halting command of English at the diction, syntactic, and idiomatic levels. Students, of course, are hardly equipped to make such fine distinctions and tend to blame their difficulties on the "funny accent." When we hear such complaints, we go to the classes and try to make the distinctions that need to be made. Pure "AC" problems should not be corrected; students need to acquire more flexible ears. But when an instructor's command of English just is not adequate, advanced ESL classes should be required.

Part Three: Appendix B: Editing and Proofreading

Chapter 18
Answers to Editing and Proofreading Practices

Editing Practice (Page 668; Page 262 Brief)

Aside from saving money, legalizing drugs would make the United States a safer place to live. Much of what the media has termed "drug-related" violence is really prohibition-related violence, including random shootings and murders associated with black-market transactions. Studies indicate that drug users, in order to maintain their habit, commit an estimated four million offenses per year totaling $7.5 billion in stolen property. That is at least 40% of all property crime in this country.

Editing Practice (Page 673; Page 267 Brief)

1. The affluent, educated, liberated women of the First World, who can enjoy freedoms unavailable to any women ever before, do not feel as free as they want to. And they can no longer restrict to the subconscious their sense that this lack of freedom has something to do with—with apparently frivolous issues, things that really should not matter. Many are ashamed to admit that such trivial concerns—to do with physical appearance, bodies, faces, hair, clothes—matter so much. But in spite of shame, guilt, and denial, more and more women are wondering if it isn't that they are entirely neurotic alone but rather that something important is indeed at stake that has to do with the relationship between female liberation and female beauty.

    —Naomi Wolf

81

2.   Students may know what AIDS is and how it is transmitted, but most are not concerned about AIDS and do not perceive themselves to be at risk. But college age heterosexuals are the number one high risk group for this disease (Gray and Sacarino 258). "Students already know about AIDS. Condom distribution, public or not, is not going to help. It just butts into my personal life," said one student surveyed. College is a time for exploration and that includes the discovery of sexual freedom. Students, away from home and free to make their own decisions for maybe the first time in their lives, have a "bigger than life" attitude. The thought of dying is the farthest from their minds. Yet at this point in their lives, they are most in need of this information.

Editing Practice (Page 675; Page 269 Brief)

When people believe that their problems can be solved, they tend to get busy solving them.

On the other hand, when people believe that their problems are beyond solution, they tend to position themselves so as to avoid blame. Take the woeful inadequacy of education in the predominantly black central cities. Does the black leadership see the ascendancy of black teachers, school administrators, and politicians as an asset to be used in improving those dreadful schools? Rarely. You are more likely to hear charges of white abandonment, white resistance to integration, conspiracies to isolate black children, even when the schools are officially desegregated. In short, white people are accused of being responsible for the problem. But if the youngsters manage to survive those awful school systems and achieve success, leaders want to claim credit. They don't hesitate to attribute that success to the glorious Civil Rights movement.

Proofreading Practice (Page 680; Page 274 Brief)

The citizens of Zurich, Switzerland ① tired of problems associated with drug abuse, experimented with legalization. The plan was to open a central park, Platzspitz, where drugs and drug use would be permitted. Many European experts felt ② that it was the illegal drug business rather than the actual use of drugs that had caused many of the cities ③ problems. While the citizens had hoped to isolate the drug problem, foster rehabilitation, and curb the AIDS epidemic, ④ the actual outcome of the Platzspitz experiment did not create the desired results. Instead, violence increased. Drug-related deaths doubled. And drug users were drawn ⑤ from not only all over Switzerland, but from all over Europe as well. With thousands of discarded syringe packets lying around, one can only speculate as to whether the spread of AIDS was curbed. The park itself was ruined ⑥ and finally on February 10, 1992, it was barred up and closed. ⑦ After studying the Swiss peoples' ⑧ experience with Platzspitz, it is hard to believe that some advocates of drug legalization in the United States are urging us to participate in the same kind of experiment.

1. Needs a comma. Past participle needs to be set off at both ends.
2. No comma. Reading the sentence aloud should show that there is no pause here.
3. Incorrect possessive. (city's)
4. Delete underlined words. They cannot be the subject or *agent* of the action "create the desired results." **Correction:** the experiment did not have the desired results.
5. Paired construction is not parallel. A correct version would be: were drawn not only from all over Switzerland but from all over Europe.
6. Comma should precede a coordinator that introduces a second main clause.
7. Dangling present participle. A correct version would be: A study of the Swiss people's experience with Platzspitz makes it hard to believe that . . . .
8. Incorrect possessive. (people's)